Praise for Post Traumatic Slave Syndrome

Dr. Joy DeGruy is a priceless asset to us all. She has lifted the bandages from the 400 year-old abscess of slavery that remains un-healed. Many black and white Americans have been taught that slavery ended by legislative means in 1865 – so the issue is neatly side-stepped in school curricula, print and broadcast media. However, the hallmark of classroom teaching and responsible journalism must be proper context – for full understanding. The removal of the slave shackle is important, but what about the emotional damage suffered by the enslaved?

Dr. DeGruy has raised this argument brilliantly, for years, lecturing far and wide. Her many appearances on my program, Like It Is, have evoked huge audience reactions from our viewers. Many have told me how coming to understand Dr. DeGruy's message on "Post T____ Slave Syndrome" has helped them grap| problems today. I share those feelings o

Now Dr. DeGruy has set down her high____ ____age/ thesis in print. And so, to quote this wondrous physician: "Let the healing begin."

-Gil Noble, Producer and Host, Like It Is, WABC_TV

Dr. Joy DeGruy's Post Traumatic Slave Syndrome: America's Legacy of Enduring Injury and Healing is a masterwork. Her deep understanding, critical analysis, and determination to illuminate core truths are essential to addressing the long-lived devastation of slavery. Her book is the balm we need to heal ourselves and our relationships. It is a gift of wholeness.

-Susan Taylor, Editorial Director, Essence Magazine

Dr. DeGruy's book is seminal research in the field of differential cross-cultural diagnosis for mental health. Cultural Competence is a requirement for mental health and behavioral science workers. This text is required reading for all learners and practitioners. It is a vast reservoir of the how, why what, when, and where for much of the enduring injury and psychic pain of African Americans. This text moves us beyond deficit modeling and pathology; it opens a window to innovative models for healing in our multi-ethnic, pluralistic and linguistically diverse society.

-Edwin J. Nichols, Ph.D. Clinical/Industrial Psychologist.

At last, the book that all people who are truly interested in understanding the lingering psychological and social impact of enslavement on Africans and Europeans has arrived. It is no exaggeration to say that Dr. DeGruy's Post Traumatic Slave Syndrome will mark a milestone in the understanding of the relationship between racism and slavery. Read this book again and again and then give it to your friends, family and colleagues who want to understand how the ghost of slavery haunts us all.

-Dr. Ray Winbush, Institute for Urban Research, Morgan State University

Dr. DeGruy's mesmerizing, riveting book is vital reading for our time. The corrosive residue on unmitigated and unrelieved atrocities called chattel slavery scours out the very core of our national identity. Neither the descendants of chattel slavery nor its designers have been unscathed. One – doomed to mythologize its meaning, the other - to turn searing pain into self-loathing. We ignore our history at our own peril. With Dr. DeGruy's potent words we can and will heal.

-Adeliade L. Sanford, Vice Chancellor, Board of Regents, State of New York

Post Traumatic Slave Syndrome:

America's Legacy of Enduring Injury and Healing

By

Joy DeGruy, Ph.D.

Foreword by Randall Robinson

Post Traumatic Slave Syndrome:
America's Legacy of Enduring Injury and Healing

by Joy DeGruy, Ph.D.

Published by
Joy DeGruy Publications Inc.
1526 NE Alberta St. #210, Portland OR 97211
www.joydegruy.com

Originally published in hardcover by Uptone Press in 2005.

DeGruy, Joy
Post Traumatic Slave Syndrome: America's Legacy
of Enduring Injury and Healing

Includes bibliographical references and index
ISBN: 978-0-9852172-0-4
LCCN: 2005927853

Printed in the United States of America

This book is dedicated to the memory of my parents Oscar and Nellie DeGruy, who provided me with the foundation that has enabled me to realize my potential and whose love and toil helped to mold and shape the person that I have become. This work is the 'fruit' of their labor.

Post Traumatic Slave Syndrome:

America's Legacy of Enduring Injury and Healing

Table of Contents

Foreword

African-Americans are being urged, not only by the traditional bastions of American power, but by many "successful" blacks as well, to forget slavery, to forget Jim Crow, to forget about all that Africa was prior to the advent of trans-Atlantic slavery.

In this far-sighted and thoughtful book, Joy DeGruy adds her voice to those who are telling black Americans to pay no attention to such disastrous advice. Inasmuch as African-Americans are the only Americans whose forebears were dragooned to America against their will and enslaved in America for nearly three centuries, a curiosity about our past, questions about ancestors known and unknown, and a need to know about Africa before we were torn from its breast is not only normal, but, indeed, is a sign of a healthy intellect, psyche, and soul.

We travel many roads with Dr. DeGruy in this work, one of the most moving of which takes us to Ndebele in Southern Africa in 1994, where we meet Ndebele children. During this visit, we gain important insights into the impact of American slavery on "our culture and our soul." The contrasts in the demeanor, attitudes, and personalities of Ndebele children, reared in traditional African societies, grounded in African traditions and mores, shaped by their own culture, on the one hand, and the children of Onverwagt, a community of blacks first enslaved and then discarded, by white South Africans, is instructive. Here we are helped to better understand the long formative influence of American slavery upon the socio-psychological dilemmas of America today, more than one hundred years after slavery's "official" abolishment.

Dr. DeGruy's essential thesis is that slavery, that most brutal and lucrative of American institutions, is a historical watershed event regarding which black Americans would be loathe (and dangerously ill-served) to soften memory, but toward which they should, indeed, purposefully stride as an area of rigorous study and research. This is essential for us to better understand and master the facts surrounding slavery as a many-tentacled institution. It is only through an appreciation of the full reality of American slavery that black Americans will understand, first, the enormity of the crime, and, secondly, that as descendents of the enslaved, we have nothing to be ashamed of.

American slavery was the economic cornerstone on which American wealth and power were built - wealth and power which lasts to this day, as do the psycho-social consequences of American slavery, both for the descendents of the enslaved as well as the descendents of the enslavers. Dr. DeGruy helps us to understand the multi-faceted impact of slavery on black life - how we relate to the world, as well as how we relate to each other. Most importantly, in this work Joy DeGruy urges us to know and embrace our past in all its fullness, for therein lies our only hope for a healthy, self-affirming present – and future.

Randall Robinson

Post Traumatic Slave Syndrome:

America's Legacy of Enduring

Injury and Healing

Prologue

Kasserian Ingera?: And How are the Children?

Among the most accomplished and fabled tribes in Africa, no tribe was considered to have warriors more fearsome or more intelligent than the mighty Masai. It is perhaps surprising then to learn the traditional greeting that passed between Masai warriors. "Kasserian ingera," one would always say to another. It means, "And how are the children?"

It is still the traditional greeting among the Masai, acknowledging the high value that the Masai always place on their childrens' well-being. Even warriors with no children of their own would always give the traditional answer. "All the children are well." Meaning, of course, that peace and safety prevail, that the priorities of protecting the young, the powerless are in place, that Masai society has not forgotten its reason for being, its proper functions and responsibilities. "All the children are well," means that life is good. It means that the daily struggles of existence even among a poor people, do not preclude proper caring for its young.

I wonder how it might affect our consciousness of our own children's welfare if in our culture we took to greeting each other with this same daily question: "And how are the children?" I wonder if we heard that question and passed it along to each other a dozen times a day, if it would begin to make a difference in the reality of how children are thought of or cared for in this country . . . I wonder if we could truly say without any hesitation, "The children are well, yes, all the children are well.

Excerpted from a speech by The Rev. Dr. Patrick T. O'Neill, First Parish Unitarian Universalist Church, Framingham, MA.

So, how are the children?

Throughout recorded history people have subjugated, enslaved and at times even exterminated one another. Sometimes these acts were committed in the name of a king or queen, other times in the name of a tribe or country. Often they were committed in the name of God. Always they were done to consolidate and expand the power of a select few. Always vast numbers of people died for no good reason. Always even a greater number of people needlessly suffered to sate the appetites of that select group. These are crimes against humanity, and these crimes continue to be executed across our planet to this day.

These crimes are perpetrated in a seemingly never-ending cycle. The powerful oppress the less powerful who, in turn oppress those even less powerful than they. These cycles of oppression leave scars on the victims and victors alike, scars that embed themselves in our collective psyches and are passed down through generations, robbing us of our humanity. For who can be truly human under the weight of oppression that condemns them to a life of torment, robs them of a future, and saps their free will? Moreover, who can become truly human when they gain so much from the pain and suffering of those whom they oppress and/or take advantage of?

Many say these conditions are part and parcel of the human condition. Perhaps they are. But every so often a Gandhi or a Mandela graces our planet and helps their people break the cycle for a time. The time has now come to follow their lead, break the cycle and once again claim our humanity. Breaking this cycle and claiming our humanity will require much work from all of us. Those who have been the victims of years, decades and centuries of oppression first must heal from injuries received first-hand, as well as those passed down through the ages. Those who have been the perpetrators of these unspeakable crimes, and those who continue to benefit from those crimes, have to honestly confront their deeds and heal from the psychic wounds that come with being the cause and beneficiaries of such great pain and suffering.

The work to be done is particular to each cultural group, whether that group's culture arose somewhere in Africa, Europe, the Americas, Asia or the Pacific Islands, and whether that group's members were victims, perpetrators, or both. The nature of this work is such that each group first must see to their own healing, because no group can do another's work. With this understanding I have dedicated my life to helping the children of the African Diaspora, particularly those whose history is wrapped up in the history of America. Hence the book before you. No, all the children are not well . . . yet. But yes, they can be.

Introduction

SANKOFA

("Return and Get It")

We must return and claim our past in order to move toward our future. It is in understanding who we were that will free us to embrace who we now are. (The meaning of Sankofa)

In the summer of 1994 my sister, my niece and I were among nine African American women that traveled to Southern Africa together. Upon my return I found it difficult to adjust to being back in Portland, Oregon, a city once touted as being the "whitest" city in America. My six-week journey throughout Southern Africa had left an indelible mark on my heart and soul.

I sat in my living room reminiscing about the villages in Lesotho: the sweetness of the children, their level of generosity, and their well-mannered behavior. We were always treated kindly and offered food and drink even when there was barely enough for one person, let alone guests. This reminded me of how my mother always used to feed what seemed to be the whole neighborhood. She had taught my brothers, my sister and I that there was always enough food to share.

Now I was back home trying to re-assimilate into my daily routines. My difficulty achieving this caused considerable concern among some of the women who were on the trip. They had begun calling my sister, asking, "Has Joy left the house yet?"

My many years as a mental health clinician at least assured me that I wasn't 'nuts.' I simply needed time to adjust to having been in a place where, for the first time, it felt perfectly normal to be black. It felt odd returning to America, to a place where being black is frequently a life sentence of cultural isolation and social invisibility.

My reminiscing was abruptly cut short when my nine-year-old daughter came racing into the room. She was out of breath and quite panicked about a situation that was happening outside, in front of the house.

"There's a boy outside who's threatening to beat up Nadim (her brother), and he says he's going to pee on our car too!" she said as she tried to catch her breath.

Well, I was finally going to have to get out of the house. I walked out onto a scene of several young black boys standing in the middle of the street. They looked to be around 10 or 11 years old. They were facing my son who stood alone. I identified the boy standing directly in front of my son as the instigator and asked, "Is there something that my son has done that you would like to tell me about?"

The young, rather stout and angry little boy responded, "Wha' he starin' at?"

"Excuse me?" I said, "What did you say?"

And the boy repeated, " I wanna know wha' he starin' at? Does he got some kinda eyeball problem?"

I was a little startled but I managed to ask, "Are you saying to me that you want to beat my son into the ground because he was looking at you?"

The young man seemed a bit uneasy with my question, hesitated and responded, "Yeah, wha' he think he lookin' at?"

I paused for a moment considering what he had said and then responded, "My son may have been looking at you because he thought that you might want to play some basketball." (In front of our house we have a hoop.) "He may have been looking at you because he was thinking of asking you if you'd like to play one of his video games in the house. He could have been looking at you because he thought that maybe you might want to walk down the street to the park."

The little boy looked to be rather overwhelmed by my statements as if to say, 'Whoa lady, it's not that deep!' I guess it was the therapist in me that got out of control. I eventually managed to settle things down by giving the boys my canned spiel, explaining how important it is for African Americans living in the 'hood' not to fight and to keep each other safe. He seemed to buy it enough to agree not to beat up my son, much to Nadim's relief.

After the boys walked away it dawned on me that there was a stark contrast between this experience and the ones in South Africa where the young African males greeted each other with the common phrase, "I see you." I couldn't help feeling the emotional distance that separated the two statements: the friendly acknowledgment, "I see you," and the angry, menacing, "What you lookin' at?" The gap between Africans and African Americans was suddenly stark and clear. Somewhere along the way African American children have become so emotionally fragile that they cannot often withstand the implications associated with a simple gaze.

I went back inside and continued thinking about what had just happened. As I sat in my living room I recalled other incidents that at the time I had thought to be nothing out of the ordinary. In considering how we as humans arrive at our self-concept or self-esteem, this statement sums up the role that significant others play in our sense of worth. 'I am not who I think that I am, and I am not who you think that I am. I am who I think that you think that I am.' What has happened to this little boy's ego integrity? And why was he so mad at my son, who is black like him? My belief is that the little boy does not hold the same anger towards white people because they do not know who he is, nor can they really see who he is. He was, however, mad at black people like my son, who can see the emptiness in him, his 'vacant esteem.' His question, "What you lookin' at?" implied that whatever he thought that my son was lookin' at was worthy of him beating Nadim bloody for it.

Now, in the light of my experiences in Africa, I began to re-examine other events involving African Americans that I previously had taken for granted. I recalled being at a local school parents' meeting where I overheard a conversation occurring between two mothers. One of the mothers was black and the other white. Their children were classmates and played sports together at school. The black mother commented on the achievements of the white mother's child, saying, "Your son is really coming along."

The white mother responded with pride, "Thank you. He is quite the man. He's in the talented and gifted program here at the school, and as you know, he's playing well in little league. He has really excelled this year! He's just like his father."

The white mother went on for some time singing the praises of her child. When she finished she turned her attention to the black mother's child, remembering how exceptional he was, and said, "Your son is also doing quite well. I hear . . ."

Before she finished her statement the black mother, who too was clearly proud of her little boy, said, "Oh girl, he's such a mess at home. Sometimes I could just strangle him."

Then there was the time at the local bank. When I arrived I noticed there were lots of people in line waiting to see a teller. There was a black mother in the bank with three small children. The children were standing close to their mother, so close in fact, they were actually holding on to her legs. Occasionally, one of the children would become curious about something or someone in the bank and attempt to explore the object or person. However, any effort to leave the mother's side resulted in a sharp verbal chastisement and a snap of her fingers to immediately 'get back to her side.'

In the same line, towards the back, there was another mother standing in line waiting for an available teller, only she was white. The white mother also had several small children close in age to the black mother's children. The mother had her hands full trying to stay in line while her little boy wandered about skipping, twirling, rolling on the floor and asking questions of the bank security guard. The white mother did not insist that her children stand by her side. Instead, she tried to keep an eye on them and apologized to the people in line who her children were annoying.

I remembered when I was a child being in a bank and other places of business with my mother and experiencing the same phenomenon of watching the white kids play while my mother insisted that I stay near her. Watching the repeat of my experience, I wondered how the little black girl who stood in the bank line felt while she watched the white boy run and play in the bank. I suspect she felt a number of emotions: fear of the consequences she might receive from disobeying her mother; shame from the curious looks of her white peers; anger at not being able to move about freely.

Without explicitly saying so, the black mother sent a message to her children and the message was, 'little white children can safely run and play but you cannot because it is not okay or safe for you.' These experiences teach black children that somehow this world does not belong to black boys and girls, but it does belong to the little white children.

Eventually a teller became available and the black mother approached the counter. This was the perfect time for the little black girl to escape. She began sliding down the length of the counter hidden from her mother's sight because she was just small enough to fit underneath the overarching counter. It was then that the little black girl felt free to explore, a natural tendency for children at her developmental stage, but she was faced with another dilemma. There was another black mother waiting in line that saw her down beneath the counter and out of her mother's vision.

Then the other black mother did something that is all too familiar to African American children: She gave the little attempted escapee the 'black mother's death stare' and gestured with a slight move of her head for her to return to her mother's side. The little black girl immediately recognized the signal, looked defeated, lowered her head, and reluctantly returned to her mother's side. The black woman in line smiled contentedly because she had successfully assisted the black mother by non-verbally reinforcing the unspoken rule that little black children cannot move about and stray. This was not a place for them to explore. Moreover, it is a world that belongs to the little white boys and girls and those like them who freely and contentedly may stroll about banks and other places of importance, oblivious to any possible restraint or limitation that may be imposed upon them.

On another occasion I was one of several hundred African Americans attending a cultural recognition ceremony when I heard people commenting on how someone they knew had just gotten a promotion. What began as a simple compliment ended up with, "You know the only real reason she got that promotion was because the manager played ball with her father."

Later on I overheard another person seated at the table comment on how her friend recently bought a new home. Again, I heard, "They can't really afford that house. Just wait and see, they're going to lose it in no time."

My kids would call these people 'haters,' folks that find it necessary to undermine the achievements of others.

In a larger context, African American organizations often fall victim to similar undermining behaviors. Many black organizations, particularly nonprofit entities, experience struggles over leadership. Here is a familiar scenario: A small grassroots program that serves elders has been developed in the community. In this particular organization the leadership duties have been divided among the three co-founders' and, like many such organizations, they have been working hard to raise the few dollars that they can. They apply for and receive a sizeable government grant. The money arrives with guidelines specifying the need for a single leader to be identified, closely followed by the three co-founders' question, "Who is going to run it?"

Now the bitter infighting begins. Cliques form and lines are drawn within the organization. Individuals that have worked closely and harmoniously suddenly become competitors. Of course in the end there really is no winner. Their quality of service declines and the level of divisiveness and distrust this 'competition' engenders plays into the expectations and views of the broader community.

Within the neighborhood criticisms are heard: "They cannot handle it." "They'll never be able to manage all that money and pull it off." Subsequently, the organization loses sight of their original purpose and, in turn, the respect of those they intended to serve.

Innocent and angry little boys threatened by a glance; proud parents reluctant to praise their children and feeling the need to inhibit their natural exploratory instincts; friends not being able to celebrate the successes of their peers; organizations torn asunder from within . . . and there's more. Parents feeling the need to protect their children from the police. Issues of skin color and hair texture continuing to dominate discussions regarding beauty and physical preference. The excessive focus on material accumulation. People needing, wanting and dreaming, yet fearing they will not succeed. Most of all frustration. Frustration and anger, at times even rage, feelings that seem to dominate many of our lives.

If you're black and living in America, none of this may be news to you. Contemporary social scientists might offer an explanation as to why an African American boy might feel disrespected by a peer that simply looks at him. They may suggest that television, newspapers and magazines projecting negative images of black males as pitiable, ignorant, violent and criminal have contributed to the overall poor self-images of black boys. Black scholars might even point out that music videos and movies depicting masculine and feminine beauty neatly wrapped in fine white features and straight hair have further deteriorated the self-images of black boys and girls, causing them to despise the reflection in the mirror.

And they would be right. However, what is not often addressed is the role our history has played in producing these negative perceptions, images and behaviors. We rarely look to our history to understand how African Americans adapted their behavior over centuries in order to survive the stifling effects of chattel slavery, effects which are evident today. I believe that the behaviors in the scenarios described above, as well as many others, are in large part related to trans-generational adaptations associated with the past traumas of slavery and on-going oppression. I have termed this condition 'Post Traumatic Slave Syndrome,' or PTSS.

So what is trauma? Trauma is an injury caused by an outside, usually violent, force, event or experience. We can experience this injury physically, emotionally, psychologically, and/or spiritually. Traumas can upset our equilibrium and sense of well-being. If a trauma is severe enough it can distort our attitudes and beliefs. Such distortions often result in dysfunctional behaviors, which can in turn produce unwanted consequences. If one traumatic experience can result in distorted attitudes, dysfunctional behaviors and unwanted consequences, this pattern is magnified exponentially when a person repeatedly experiences severe trauma, and it is much worse when the traumas are caused by human beings.

The slave experience was one of continual, violent attacks on the slave's body, mind and spirit. Slave men, women and children were traumatized throughout their lives and the violent attacks during slavery persisted long after emancipation. In the face of these injuries, those traumatized adapted their attitudes and behaviors to simply survive, and these adaptations continue to manifest today. Post Traumatic Slave Syndrome examines these adaptations with an eye towards identifying, today, those that limit us and those that make us stronger.

Now, viewed through the historical lens of slavery and its aftermath, one may better understand the hesitancy of African American mothers to acknowledge the fine qualities of their children. When we roll the scene back a few hundred years we see a slave master walking through the fields coming upon a slave woman. The slave master approaches her and her children and remarks, "Well now, that Mary of yours is really coming along."

The slave mother, terrified that the slave master may see qualities in her daughter that could merit her being raped or sold, says, "Naw sir, she ain't worth nothin'. She cain't work. She stupid. She shiftless."

The slave mother's denigrating statements about her daughter were spoken in an effort to dissuade the slave master from molesting or selling her, and of course, no one would fault her. This behavior was nothing special. Slave mothers and fathers had been belittling their children in an effort to protect them for hundreds of years. Yet what originally began as an appropriate adaptation to an oppressive and danger-filled environment has been subsequently transmitted down through generations.

It is evidenced today by behaviors like those exhibited by the black woman at the school meeting. While on the surface seemingly harmless, such behavior serves to both humiliate and injure the young black children of today, who cannot understand why their mothers and fathers, who are obviously proud of them, speak so poorly of them. All too often these children actually begin to internalize the demeaning criticisms. Furthermore, these criticisms create feelings of being disrespected by the very people that they love and trust the most, their parents. It is not hard to imagine the impact of these painful, vilifying remarks on the self-esteem of many black children, especially when one considers the years of repetition. Sadly, neither the black mother nor her children understand the historical forces that have helped to shape her behavior.

With the same historical lens, one can better understand why the mother in the bank insisted that her children be near her. In the slave environment, and continuing through reconstruction and the long night of Jim Crow, it was inherently unsafe for a black child to stray, wander or question white people. Such behavior could result in severe punishment or even death. Thus, black slaves were hyper-vigilant about the whereabouts of their children, for such hyper-vigilance meant survival.

It is equally understandable why an African American might feel threatened by the accomplishments of a peer when viewed in the light of slavery. Slaves were divided in many different respects; masters distinguished the house slave from the field slave, the mulatto from the black slave, etc. Often these different designations meant access to, or denial of, privileges and sometimes freedom itself. It was common practice for slave owners to set one class of slave against another. Slave owners perpetuated feelings of separateness and distrust by sometimes ordering black overseers to beat or punish their friends, peers and relatives. When the master 'promoted' a slave, that slave often joined the master in the rank of "oppressor."

. These are just a few examples of behaviors that have roots in slavery and have been passed down through generations. Most of them ensured our survival at one time or another. Some of them will inhibit our ability to survive and thrive today if they are not brought to light, examined, and where necessary, replaced with behaviors which promote and maximize our progress.

The primary purpose of this book is to encourage African Americans to view their attitudes, assumptions and behaviors through the lens of history and so gain a greater understanding of the impact centuries of slavery and oppression has had on our lives. With this understanding we can explore the role our history has played in the evolution of our thoughts and feelings about who and what we are, as well as our beliefs about how we are to behave. While it is true that some of this evolution has resulted in behaviors that have become both destructive and maladaptive, it is also encouraging that in spite of the oppressive conditions our ancestors endured, they were able to pass on their phenomenal powers of resilience and adaptability. It is essential that we build upon these strengths in ways that will sustain and advance future generations. In this way we can begin the healing.

Chapter 1:

"I Don't Even Notice Race"

Racism, one of the most baneful and persistent evils, is a major barrier to peace. Its practice perpetrates too outrageous a violation of the dignity of human beings to be countenanced under any pretext. Racism retards the unfoldment of the boundless potentialities of its victims, corrupts its perpetrators, and blights human progress. Recognition of the oneness of mankind, implemented by appropriate legal measures, must be universally upheld if this problem is to be overcome.

The Bahá'í Universal House of Justice, 1985

I arrived in South Africa in 1994 on the heels of the inauguration of President Nelson Mandela. As an African American, sharing the same black skin of those impacted by Apartheid I set off prepared to face opposition and shunning by disgruntled white South Africans. My preparation resembled how one might respond after a run-in, perhaps a little flare up, a few harsh words with a co-worker on a Friday afternoon. You know that you're going to see that person the following week so you mentally 'plan' for Monday. You may say to yourself, 'Well you know, if they come in and they say that, this is what I'm going to say.' You get the idea.

So I had kind of a chip on my shoulder as I left Portland. Upon my arrival in South Africa I was warmly greeted and enjoyed several uneventful weeks. In other words, I didn't have a single negative encounter. So, I started to provoke people. I wasn't about to return home from South Africa without having had a real deep kind of 'experience' to recount. So I would approach white South Africans and I'd say,

"Tell me a little bit about that apartheid, huh? What was that like?"

On numerous occasions they'd answer by saying, " Yes Joy, it was an awful experience, the oppression of the blacks, the behavior of the whites. Glad its over though. Welcome to the new South Africa."

Somewhat puzzled by these responses, I decided to ask some black South Africans. So I'd go up to the black South Africans and say,

"So tell me a little about that apartheid. It must have been awful."

They'd say, "Yeah Joy, it was awful, the oppression of the blacks, the behavior of the whites. Glad its over though. Welcome to the new South Africa."

I was shocked and thought to myself, 'Isn't anybody upset here in South Africa?' Even we have our disgruntled folks back in America. You know, like the Neo-Nazis in Idaho! It later occurred to me, that in the six weeks that I had spent traveling throughout Southern Africa, I had never felt the level of racial tension that I experienced at home in the United States. I had experienced more tension during the brief time that I was in the Portland airport preparing to leave, than I did throughout the entire time I had spent in Southern Africa.

I had to ask myself, what am I observing in this experience? Why was there so little racial tension in South Africa, a country with the fresh, open wounds of Apartheid? And why so much racial tension in America, a country that ended its great sin of chattel slavery well over a hundred years ago, and its version of Apartheid almost 38 years prior to my visit to southern Africa? Perhaps South Africans experience so little tension

· compared to Americans because officially Apartheid had such a short life span, about 45 years. Perhaps it is because in the end they voluntarily gave up their unjust system. Perhaps it is because South Africa admitted their crimes to the world and, with the Truth and Reconciliation Hearings, many whites in South Africa owned up to the crimes they committed against their black countrymen.

Whatever the reasons, it is clear America has chosen a very different approach. I believe the ever-present racial tension in America is just one of the manifestations of our most serious illness: racism. Racism has run like poison through the blood of American society since Europeans first landed on these shores. And, since that beginning, America and Americans have invested much in denying it. America's and Americans' denial of their blatant racism and the attending atrocities committed throughout the nation's history has become pathological. Such denial has allowed this illness to fester for almost 400 years. It is what keeps this country sick with this issue of race.

At the root of this sickness is the unchallenged belief that there are physical differences between people that account for the intellectual attributes and abilities of those people. Since before the time of Aristotle people have been using this idea of racial difference to justify the subjugation and enslavement of those different and less powerful than themselves. Such brutality and oppression in the name of racial superiority has occurred so many times, over so many years, that we can no longer recognize and acknowledge the simple beauty in the diversity of the human family.

Today the concept 'race' has gotten confused with variation in physical appearance and cultural expression. This confusion has led to our inability to identify this simple beauty as evidenced by people proudly saying, "I don't notice race." This is particularly unfortunate because we now know that 'race,' in the way most people have come to understand it, is as valid a notion as the earth being flat.

The Myth of Race

Here's a little test. What are the races of humanity? Perhaps you came up with a list that looks like this, using identification by colors:

Black, white, brown, yellow, red.

Or maybe you are more politically correct, and your list may have looked like this:

African, European, Asian, Native American Hispanic/Latino, Pacific Islander.

Or perhaps you're really, really reaching back and came up with:

Negroid, Caucasoid and Mongoloid.

Despite our constant everyday use of the term 'race' and our reference to various races, the biology of human beings is such that there are no real differences between humans. Race is frequently characterized by skin color, hair texture, facial features, etc. These differences are offered as examples of how we differ as humans. The underlying assumption is that there is a genetic/biological component to these distinctions that defines the 'races.'

This assumption simply is not true. One cannot separate people into racial groups based upon any set of physical characteristics. Attempting to do so is fraught with contradictions. The Bushmen of Southern Africa look as much Asian as they do African. Pacific Islanders have both African and Asian features. The Ainu of Japan look more European than Asian. The Lapps of Scandinavia look as much like Eskimos as they do Europeans. The Aboriginal peoples of Australia, who often look African, commonly have very straight and wavy hair and are frequently blond as children.

These are just a few of the problems one runs into when arguing for the existence of biological racial differences. There are many others, among them dark-skinned people from India, or Egyptians who run the gamut from European-looking to African. And how do we identify those from the Middle East? There is however, hope for those who must differentiate people by race: Earwax. Yes, earwax. As far as we know it seems that east Asian peoples have dry earwax and the rest of the population has moist earwax. So if it is important to you to group people by physical characteristics, there's something you can hang your hat on.

James King author of "The Biology of Race," sums the discussion of race up best:

> *Race is a concept of society that insists there is a genetic significance behind human variations in skin color that transcends outward appearance. However, race has no scientific merit outside of sociological classifications. There are no significant genetic variations within the human species to justify the division of "races."* [1]

Unfortunately, while the notion of 'race' is illusory, the fact of racism in America is not. Whenever I ask an audience of people if they know what the term 'racism' means they almost universally say they do. I often give a little test to determine if everyone is on the same page regarding the term. I first ask my audience if whites can be racists. Of course, everybody agrees they can. I then ask if blacks can be racist and I get the same the response. I then ask them to identify the ways in which 'white racism' adversely impacts the lives of black people as a group, and a list forms.

My audience tells me blacks are impacted economically through discriminatory hiring practices. Having little or no access to capital, blacks are seen as lacking business acumen. They are impacted by limited access to health care. They are impacted by over-representation in the criminal justice system and under-representation in the university system. They are impacted by redlining and other discriminatory practices barring them from finding housing in the areas of their choice. The list goes on.

I then ask them to identify how black racism adversely impacts the lives of white people as a group and there is silence. There is silence, because while black people may have prejudices, and at times even feel hatred towards white people, perhaps even causing many fear, the reality is that black people lack the 'power' to affect the lives of white people as a group. Black people's feelings towards white people do not preclude a white person's ability to get a loan, receive fair treatment by the justice system, acquire education, etc.

This then is racism. It is the belief that people differ along biological and genetic lines and that one's own group is superior to another group. This belief is coupled with the power to negatively effect the lives of those perceived to be inferior. America's history is inextricably bound to this racist ideology. From the codifying of slavery, to the belief in its 'Manifest Destiny,' to the treatment of 'illegal immigrants,' many of America's actions continue to conflict with its creed that "All men are created equal."

America perceives itself to be the 'melting pot,' 'the land of opportunity.' The words engraved in bronze inside of the Statue of Liberty, "Give me your tired, your poor, your huddled masses yearning to breathe free, the wretched refuse of your teeming shore. Send these, the homeless, tempest-tossed to me," might lead one to believe all have been welcomed to the shores of America as people with equal rights, privileges, and most importantly, prospects for success.

To be sure, by and large, many immigrants have found this to be true. Western and Northern Europeans in the 19th Century, Eastern and southern Europeans early in the 20th Century all came, experienced their hardships and within a few decades were enjoying their version of the American dream. Currently, Asian immigrants and others are proceeding along a similar path. America has been and continues to be promoted as a nation which prides itself on equal opportunity as well as a rich multiculturalism.

However, history has told a divergent story where Africans are concerned. With the endorsement of slavery as a legal, acceptable and justifiable institution, the founding fathers committed America's original sin, a sin that has continued to plague America. Allowing slavery to persist at America's inception caused those who signed off on the sentiments so eloquently represented in their Declaration of Independence to perjure themselves in its face and doom the nation to a future of lies, pain and struggle.

Since that time black America has labored to recover from the dehumanization of bondage, the offense of peonage, the outrage of the black codes, the affront of convict leasing, the indignities of Jim Crow and the ravages of poverty. During the same time white America has struggled to come to grips with its legacy of chattel slavery and other crimes it committed in the name of morality, progress and supremacy. The behaviors associated with maintaining and justifying slavery, as well as the consequent assault on the generations of African Americans that followed, has resulted in yet unmeasured injury to the American psyche. America's resistance to accepting its responsibility for slavery and repairing the damage done, continue to prevent the nation from taking its place as the world's moral leader.

So, we need to 'notice' race as it relates to differential treatment because the relationship between blacks and whites continues to be among the most challenging issues facing the country today. The problems engendered by race are seemingly intractable. The distrust many black people have for whites is often palpable. The indifference of most whites to the black experience is contemptible. The disparities with regard to health, wealth and education are vast and expanding. All of these things make it more difficult to live as a black person in America than as a white person.

We need to 'notice' because the overarching problem of this millennium continues to be the problem of the color line. Almost one hundred and fifty years after emancipation and more than fifty years after *Brown vs. The Board of Education* segregation remains the norm rather than the exception. Issues of race and diversity are so critical because they remain at the root of the most pervasive problems facing this nation.

We also need to 'notice' because so little understanding exists between black and white America. On the face of it we are at best civil with each other, but all too often this civility masks unresolved resentments and hatreds. African Americans are repeatedly asked to reveal 'proof' of the realities of racism to skeptical white people. They reluctantly explain the countless incidents of discrimination, and even assaults directed at them and those they love. More often than not, the response of the questioner is denial and disbelief. The black person, having reopened wounds, is left frustrated and reinjured.

To me, noticing difference is most important because it is the first step in arresting the national hemorrhaging of African Americans. It is through such an awareness that we can take the first steps towards healing the wounds passed on to the present generation by centuries of ignorance and neglect at the hands of the governors and the governed alike.

And this is not only between black and white America. We need to notice because the overwhelming majority of the world are people of color. So if humanity is to evolve we need to notice the differences among peoples, understand them, celebrate them, learn how to integrate these differences and become a true world community.

The Emergence of African American Culture

So as race plays little or no role in describing the differences between peoples, culture plays a highly significant one. During the 1980's, 'diversity' became important in America and culture began to be celebrated in our schools. Most often that meant a discussion about cuisine, holidays and attire. Twenty years later little has changed. When people think of 'celebrating diversity,' most think of food and festival experiences. Occasionally people will include language in the mix. These are indeed diverse aspects of cultures; however, they barely scratch the surface. There are many much more significant differences. The most important of these are so deeply rooted in our psyches that most of us don't even know they exist and so rarely, if ever, do we examine them. Dr. Edwin Nichols, in his seminal work, "The Philosophical Aspects of Cultural Difference," explores some of these differences. It is Dr. Nichols' framework that lays the foundation for the following discussion.

Imagine you have a meeting scheduled for 9:00 at your place of business. About 30 people are expected to show up. It might be some kind of departmental planning meeting or a monthly meeting to get everyone up to speed on new policies. Now imagine you are 20 minutes late for this meeting. When you arrive the meeting is already in progress. What do you do?

If you are like most Americans you enter the room as inconspicuously as possible, take a seat in the back, and quietly get caught up. Hopefully no one will notice. If someone does notice you and points out your tardiness, you respectfully apologize, then quietly sit down.

In many parts of Africa things are very different. Let me tell you about a meeting I attended in Lesotho. The meeting was scheduled for 8:00. Forty to fifty people were expected to show up. Our group got there a few minutes early and watched as everyone happily talked with each other, apparently in no particular hurry to get started. The meeting actually got started close to 9:00. About 15 minutes after the meeting had gotten under way a woman entered. Did she quietly take a seat in the back? No, she did not. Was she inconspicuous? Not at all. When she arrived the meeting came to a halt.

She first offered an apology, then everyone greeted her. "No apology is necessary." "Welcome." "It's very good to see you." "Glad you could come," all expressing happiness that she had arrived.

To my surprise she then went around the room and greeted everyone . . . individually. This went on every time a person entered the meeting, all in all about dozen times. On a few occasions the person entering gestured the meeting to continue without making the rounds. To those at the meeting it seemed as if nobody showed up 'late.' They simply showed up at another time. The meeting ended when the work was done.

This is just one example. There are literally hundreds of others. Anyone who does business overseas knows this. Every culture has a myriad of customs, mores and tacit rules that a person must be aware of if their ventures are to have a chance of succeeding. The importance of accepting hospitality in Saudi Arabia, following greeting customs in Lesotho, and showing deference in Japan are just a few illustrations.

In an even more fundamental way these customs, mores and rules flow from the value systems that are the bedrock of a particular culture. If we are to understand African American culture, we must understand the African value systems from which it sprung. Let's look at three philosophical concepts that helped to form part of the bedrock on which African American culture is based: the preeminence of relationship; our African-based conception of time; and the role traditions and intuition play in knowing the world.

Preeminence of Relationship

I remember a story told to me about two white men who shared an office for 20 years. They greeted and smiled at each other each day as they got to the office, exchanged trivialities about each other's family, golfed together, and attended all the company's social functions. They both were productive members of the corporation and worked together closely. Yet the entire time they despised each other. They talked behind each other's back, tried to undermine each other's reputation and worked to beat each other out of the next promotion. These two gentlemen worked in the same office and held those feelings all those years, yet it never impacted their ability to get their jobs done.

The two men tacitly agreed to not acknowledge their animosity or their true feelings towards each other for the sake of their main objective

– getting their paychecks. Contrast this story with what is likely to happen if both of the gentlemen described above are African American. Given the preeminent role that relationships play in African American culture, two African American men are not likely to find this situation tolerable despite the fact that they also need the paycheck. Their awareness of each other's feelings while being in such close proximity could put a strain on their working relationship. They would probably find it difficult because they could not be 'real,' i.e., authentic; for to be so could conceivably lead to a confrontation or even a physical altercation. They would be operating out of an African American socio-cultural context replete with appropriate rules and protocols. Thus, the above situation would be a violation of these rules and protocols and could lead to an unworkable condition.

In the African American community relationship frequently trumps everything else. Consideration of relationship permeates all of our interactions. For example; if black students feel they have been disrespected by a teacher, they often feel completely justified in rebelling and shutting out the offending teacher, even if it means failing the class and sabotaging their academic aspirations. Some students may go so far as to act out and wind up in the Vice Principal's office. Similarly, in the workplace where there is tension between African American workers and their co-workers or boss, the rift will often be apparent to any observer and may even impact productivity. Situations involving family or close friends will often take precedence over attendance at school, work, meetings, etc., regardless of the consequences.

While we all may be aware of the fact that some African Americans often respond, to their detriment, in the manners related above, it is also clear that these and similar behaviors at times have served to strengthen the individual and the community. It is vitally important to understand the role that relationships play in African American culture in order to differentiate between harmful/dysfunctional adaptive behaviors, and positive/functional ones.

Historically, African societies were arranged based upon kinship relationships. The extended family was an interdependent unit that provided for the care of the children, the sick and the elderly. In African culture your nieces and nephews would consider themselves brothers and sisters instead of cousins. The extended family structure was part of a survival strategy, particularly for Africans whose kinship ties provided the mechanism for child-rearing and social organization. All the members of the extended family helped to provide for the basic needs of food, clothing and shelter. Cooperation within a close-knit family insured the continued existence of the particular tribe or group. Similarly, in African American culture, not only is there an extended family, but there is also what has come to be known as 'fictive kinship,' meaning that unrelated individuals are granted the status of family by being given the names of aunt, uncle, cousin, etc. With such a title come unique rights and privileges of freely interacting within the family.

Consistent with the African focus on interpersonal relationships is the responsibility and accountability of each member of the tribe for their personal actions and behaviors. Thus, the adage, 'what goes around, comes around,' has particular meaning in the African American community. Asante, in the book *African Culture: The Rhythms of Unity*, describes the roles that relationships play in the African world view.

There was an organic view that the whole order was related in a dynamic sense. Tampering with one part was believed to affect the whole. All parts had to be in rhythm and harmony with one another leading to a sense of connection to the cosmos. Time, in traditional African culture, has been viewed as a central phenomenon. The worldview has had a religious base and has emphasized an external locus of control and the need for humans to temporarily harmonize themselves with the forces of control and the forces around them. Time has been used in establishing a complexity of balanced relationships: one, time is used to establish a relationship with the Supreme Being; two, to establish a relationship of continuity between the present and past generations; three, to establish a relationship with nature and the forces of one's environment (nature); and four, to create group harmony and participation among the living.[2]

Compatible with the principle of maintaining harmony and connectedness, much of the political arrangement of African societies was decentralized, showing little concern for control over territories. These 'stateless societies' relied principally on consensus, customs and traditions rather than legislative processes. Relying on consensus confirmed that all individuals were important in determining the movement and direction of the whole group.

African peoples consider all things in the universe dynamically related. They see the world as a balance of internal and external loci of control, a universe of interconnected spiritual and temporal networks, with which people ideally strive to synchronize themselves. Mbiti, in the book *African Religions and Philosophy*, describes this universe:

There are five divisions of the ontology, ranked in order of descending importance: (1) God, (2) spirits, (3) man, (4) animals and plants, and (5) inanimate objects. The ontology is anthropocentric in that attention is focused upon man (humans) as the center. Humans are acutely aware of their position in relation to other forms of existence since a balance must be maintained at all times and since all modes must keep their proper place and distance from each other. Unity and interdependence are crucial since an upset in one of the categories upsets the whole order. God is believed to be the creator, the sustainer, and the ultimate controller of life; Africans thus have little difficulty reconciling His intervention into the affairs of humans, even though the spirits are believed to be His emissaries.[3]

Given this view of the world, each individual is viewed as an important, integral part of the whole. Optimally this view demands that we treat each individual as of equal importance, for altering the individual consequently alters the whole. Therefore, each person, in and of himself or herself, is seen as a cherished and vital entity.

The importance of relationship manifests itself in many ways. One of the most obvious is greeting behavior. In some cultures greeting tends to be somewhat perfunctory. Often at meetings introductions will be dispensed with because of time considerations. At the foundation of African culture, in contrast, is the emphasis on relationship between individuals. The custom in Lesotho of greeting everyone who enters a meeting may appear to be impractical based on American conventions; however, it is completely appropriate given the significance that Africans place on maintaining positive regard through established relationships. Greeting becomes a symbol which underscores the importance placed on the relationship.

Such greeting is essential in African culture because it is a gesture which confirms there is a shared bond. During my lectures, I will often call upon strangers in the room, two black men from opposite corners, to approach and greet each other as a demonstration to my audiences of the pervasive cultural norm of extended greeting among African Americans. The two strangers will immediately shake hands followed by a slight embrace or any number of gestures, inclusive of finger snaps, fist to fist taps, and so forth.

If I find myself walking down the street, and I happen to catch the eye of another African American man or woman walking toward me, I will always give a customary head nod, to acknowledge that 'I see them.' And I am met with the same recognition despite the fact that we do not know each other. Greeting is just one small manifestation of the importance of acknowledging relationships.

Here's another. We were crossing the border of Lesotho in Southern Africa when we came upon an unusual sign posted outside of the customs office, which read:

WARNING!

POSSESSION OF ILLEGAL WEAPONS COULD CONDEMN YOU TO: 25 YEARS IN JAIL AND COMMUNITY AND FAMILY REJECTION
PLEASE HAND IT IN FOR THE SAKE OF YOUR COMMUNITY

Rejected by family and community? When was the last time you saw a law enforcement agency in America use that as a deterrent? I have never encountered a warning sign which included the potential negative impact such an infraction could bring on the individual's family or community. In America this would simply not be seen as a message that would deter anyone from committing a crime. Again, it serves to underscore the importance Africans place on interpersonal relationships.

Our children are no different. They place a similar emphasis on relationships. In schools all across the country teachers use material rewards to motivate their students. For many years I have worked with school districts from Portland, Oregon to Atlanta, Georgia, and it has been my experience that you can motivate white children with such rewards for a much longer time than black children. It is no surprise that the teachers that have the most success working with many students of color emphasize building strong relationships based upon mutual trust and respect.

Consider the following scenario: A second-grade teacher has created a chart with all of the pupils' names written down the left-hand side. To the right of the names are five columns indicating the days of the week. The children are told that they will receive a sticker in the shape of a star next to their name if they complete all of their seatwork for the day.

Johnny is an African American student in the class.

"Now Johnny, if you do all of your seatwork, we're going to give you a star."

Johnny completes his seatwork for Monday and replies with great excitement, "Ooooh, I got a star!"

On Tuesday, Johnny gets the same results and he again replies, "Ooooh, I got another star."

By the third day, Johnny may tell his teacher, "I can make my own stars, and I'm not doing all of that seatwork for a star."

In addition, Johnny may not complete his seat work for a smiley face, a ribbon or even a B or an A. Educators commonly fault Johnny as lacking the desire or capacity to learn. It is more likely that the material rewards offered by the teacher no longer serve as an incentive for him.

There are alternative approaches for motivating a child like Johnny. One that I have often used is to put my arm around him and say, "Johnny, now I know that you're going to get all of your seatwork done because you know I'm counting on you, and I believe that you can do a really good job." The words above suggest that I believe in Johnny and he will work for that! He will work for the 'relationship.'

Black parents sometimes find that their child is not performing academically up to his or her potential and is receiving unacceptable grades. When asked by their parents why they are receiving only a 'C,' the black child may often respond with, "It's because my teacher doesn't like me."

While this response is not likely to be met with approval by the parent, its prevalence suggests there is more to it than a rebellious student. As a parent and an educator I have had to consider the pervasiveness of this answer among African American children, teens and often college students as well. Whether or not these students accurately perceive what teachers feel towards them is less important than the fact that their teachers' feelings 'matter' at all. What it does suggest is that it is important for black students to feel well-regarded by their teachers.

Given the significance of relationships that I had learned from Nichols' work, I developed and implemented a relationship-based approach to education specifically designed for teachers who work in schools with significant populations of African American and Hispanic American students. At the heart of this culturally-based model is the establishment of strong relationships as the fundamental and essential ingredient for the academic success of these students.

Unfortunately, African American children are often treated with disdain upon entering an elementary, middle or high school. On numerous occasions I have observed the individual assigned to the front desk to be the most hostile and bitter member of the school staff. They in fact do not appear to like children at all! Consequently, many students have been emotionally assaulted before they can even get to class. This is a major problem if you accept the concept that perhaps the most effective motivator for black children is love. Clearly, other children are also highly motivated by love. The difference is in the absence of affection, some children will work for stars and points and the like. In my experience, in love's absence, those material types of rewards will not work very long as effective motivators for black children.

It is easy to underestimate the role relationships play in black culture. From fights between children in New York City's schoolyards to gang-related violence in L.A.'s streets, to tribal wars on the African continent, dysfunctional relationships often stand as the most significant factor in precipitating conflict. Correspondingly, building and maintaining healthy relationships are two of the most significant factors in facilitating peace and harmony.

It's About Time

Those who have traveled through Europe know of Germany's reputation for extraordinary exactitude. If the bus schedule says the bus to

Berlin leaves at 8:03am, that is exactly when it will leave, not 8:02 or 8:04. 8:03 on the nose. Of course, in Africa things are usually quite different. In a small village in Kenya the bus to Nairobi may leave on Tuesday. In some places in Africa planes will take off when there are enough passengers. Each culture has its own conception of time. We are not directly taught what time is nor how it works. We learn through our interactions with our respective cultures or societies.

A number of years ago a friend of mine met a man that taught English in China from 1982 to 1984. During their discussion he asked him what the Chinese people thought of Communism. After all, it had been around for more than thirty years and it must have had a huge impact on the population. His response surprised my friend at the time. He said most people he had met viewed Communism like any other dynasty; they didn't pay much attention to it because it will be gone within a couple of hundred years. Apparently, some Chinese people have a broad view of time. Americans get upset when a person they didn't vote for gets to be President for four years . . . or worse, eight years.

Underlying African behavior is a view of time as being flexible and plentiful. From the African perspective, time serves the relationships among people, hence meetings like the one I attended in Lesotho. Many gatherings in Africa tend to have indefinite starting times as well as indefinite completion times. Meetings are likely to begin when everyone has arrived and finish when the purpose has been accomplished. The European time pressure that people frequently feel in America is relatively non-existent in Africa. That rushed feeling many Americans experience is an American phenomenon. In some parts of the world people are more laid back. More time is taken for each other.

In America, black people who show up late for work are often characterized as unprofessional. To correct for the time 'lost,' an African American worker that shows up late will expect to work through their lunch hour or make up the time at the end of the day. The issue is many employers do not, or can not make the distinction between an unprofessional employee and an industrious one.

For many of us, strict adherence to time was not part of our upbringing. Throughout my childhood our home had a very loose temporal structure to it. Yes, like many families we ate dinner together every evening. However, we had no set time for dinner like in many European American households. Yes, we had to be home at a certain time, but it wasn't at 6:30; it was when the streetlights came on. Strict adherence to a clock simply did not play a particularly strong role in our lives. The result is that I adjust to the bi-cultural nature of time with a level of flexibility that allows me to smoothly move between cultures.

For some cultures time is something to be parsed, counted and measured. Time can be lost, saved and gained. It is a resource and some people have little of it while others have a lot. In other cultures time is seen as an infinite resource, a force with which they have to live. In still other cultures, like those in Africa, time is not something for us to control; it is something with which we attune ourselves. Life has a rhythm, and flowing with it is what is important.

Learning About the World

How do we come to learn about our world? We come to understand our world through many means. We use reasoning, observation and calculation. We use our five senses, and our intuition. We use symbolic imagery through stories and analogies. We use all of these and more. In order to more fully understand ourselves we need to be aware of how each of these is emphasized in African culture.

Africans and their descendants created great dynasties and empires, constructed pyramids and founded medicine. All these accomplishments necessitated considerable use of objective calculations. They also learned much through subjective approaches, relying more on intuition and natural feeling. For example: a common way of describing an event might include statements like, "I was picking up something going on in the meeting," or, "There were some heavy vibes in the room," or, "I wasn't feeling her/him." These statements reflect a group tendency to place high value on internal barometers. It is not surprising that people whose primary concern is their relationship with each other would evolve such an emphasis.

And it is this emphasis that lay at the heart of the African tradition of transmitting knowledge and wisdom through what Nichols describes as symbolic imagery. If a picture is worth a thousand words, from the African perspective the lessons that can be learned from stories and analogies are worth a thousand pictures. Throughout Africa storytellers hold an esteemed place in the community. They are the repositories of knowledge. They are the teachers. They pass down their wisdom through stories, the symbolic imagery of their life experience. This oral tradition has been passed along and is evident in African American culture today.

The importance of learning through symbolic imagery cannot be stressed enough. Today in schools across the country our children are presented with subject matter that is of little interest to them. This is primarily because our students view their schoolwork as seemingly unconnected to their lives, having little significance in their ultimate success or survival. Thus, the frequent question that comes from African American students, regardless of their age, in response to a teacher's requirements for their class is inevitably . . . why? Why are we learning this? Meaning, what does this have to do with my world or reality? When our students do not see the connection between the subject at hand and their lives, they tend to become bored and unmotivated. Conversely, they will become highly motivated and excited about learning when they do see the connections. It is through symbolic imagery that these connections can be made apparent.

Some years ago, I was teaching at a middle school. While my sixth-grade students were filing into my classroom, four white gentlemen also entered. They each carried a clipboard and pen, and seated themselves in the last row. At first I didn't pay too much attention to them as I was busy greeting each child as they came in. Only when all the students were seated did I query my unexpected guests about the purpose of their visit. One of them quickly explained that they were visiting various programs in the area that offered curricula about alcohol and drugs to determine which programs their foundation would fund. They assured me they would not be a source of interruption and encouraged me to carry on as I normally would.

I decided to give them each a copy of my pre- and post-test on amphetamines and barbiturates, which was the subject of the week's curriculum. As I turned to walk away I noticed some chuckling coming from several of them. I overheard one of them ask another if he knew the answer to one of the test questions. I found out later they were not able to answer many of the 20 questions on my test.

I then heard one of them mumble something about doubting that my students could pass the test. That was the last straw. I turned to them and stated I had no doubt whatsoever that my students, mainly consisting of hormone raging boys labeled as disruptive and low achieving, would pass the test with flying colors. What resulted has been affectionately referred to by past students as "The Story of Barbara."

The Story of Barbara

I started off by explaining to my class that I was going to be sharing a unit on the drugs amphetamines and barbiturates, and asked them to repeat after me: "**A** - amphetamines take you to the top!" and "**B** – barbiturates take you to the bottom!"

"**A** - amphetamines take you to the top!" and "**B** – barbiturates take you to the bottom!" they repeated enthusiastically.

I asked my students, "Is it safe to assume that an amphetamine had the opposite affect of a barbiturate?"

"Yes." They answered.

This would be the only reference in the way of specifics about the two drugs that would be made that day. I then began to tell a story about a real life event that occurred when I was a child growing up on 63rd and Brynhurst, two blocks west of Crenshaw Blvd. in South Central Los Angeles.

I asked my students if they knew of anyone that lived in their neighborhood that acted a little strange, someone that maybe talked to themselves or yelled or screamed at people for no apparent reason? They all commented they knew or heard about such people. I explained that I was going to tell them about someone who lived in my neighborhood that everyone knew because she was always doing something strange. Her name was Barbara. In addition to having mental challenges, Barbara was also addicted to drugs.

"Which drug might you think Barbara was addicted to?"

"Barbiturates!" they yelled out.

"Yes," I responded, "it just so happens Barbara was addicted to barbiturates."

I began my story.

When I was ten or eleven years old, a bunch of us kids were playing 'kick the can' in the middle of the street.

"What were you kicking a can for?" a couple of students asked.

This question was a clear sign I was aging! I took a moment to explain that it was just a different version of 'hide and go seek' only with a can. They seemed satisfied with the answer and I continued the story.

It was getting toward evening and as we were playing, we saw Barbara at the corner walking towards us. She was muttering and swearing as she usually did, only today she was carrying a large hammer, the kind that has a big ball on one side and a hammer head on the other. We all stopped to watch her because we knew Barbara could be unpredictable and aggressive. Parked directly in front of where we were playing was a brand new Cadillac replete with gleaming chrome, leather bucket seats and a miniature steering wheel called a 'donut,' which was quite popular back then.

We watched as Barbara took her hammer and broke every window, the windshield, the headlights, and the taillights. Barbara then climbed up on the car and continued pounding on the hood. When she was satisfied with her work she got off of the car, walked over to the apartment where the owner of the car lived, and proceeded to break every window she could reach. When she finished, she sat on the trunk of the car mumbling and swearing. We all stood perfectly still as if we were in a scene from "West Side Story." We had watched in total shock as Barbara pretty much demolished the car of a neighbor who was soon to return from work.

It seemed like only moments passed before we saw him turn the corner. He wore black hard-rimmed glasses, black work pants and a black work shirt. He was carrying the remains of his lunch in a rolled up paper bag. As he approached, Barbara began yelling profanities and spitting wildly while still sitting on the car trunk. The man walked slowly around the car as if inspecting the damage, all the while ignoring Barbara. He then turned towards his apartment, stepping carefully around the broken glass from his apartment windows.

When he went inside we all began to run for cover. In the 'hood' when someone goes into their home under these kind of conditions, they are very likely to come out with some kind of a weapon. We all scattered like birds, hiding behind cars, trees, anything we could find. It was now dark. The single street light on our block had come on but we were all too terrified to run home. I was hiding behind a large bush that was closest to the scene. Sure enough, when the man returned he grabbed Barbara from off of his car and began beating her severely.

The whispers of the hiding children could be heard coming from every direction, "Barbara really went and did it this time." "Boy, she is getting her butt kicked now." But I was silent because I could see what the rest of my young companions could not. I could see that the man was not hitting

Barbara . . . he was stabbing her. I began to shake uncontrollably. My heart felt as though it was going to beat its way out of my chest. I didn't know whether to stay hidden or try to run home because I was afraid he would see me and hurt me too. In a flash, I began running as fast as I could. It was three blocks to my house. I didn't look back, I just kept running. I jumped clear over the steps of my house onto the porch and into the house screaming for my mother. When I reached her I was out of breath, panicked and sweating. My mother saw the terror in my eyes and feared the worse. I finally got out a garbled message,

"Mama! I saw Barbara . . . broke . . . the man's car . . . he stabbed and . . . he stabbed her." My mother immediately called the paramedics. They and the police finally arrived thirty minutes later.

I stopped the story at this point and asked my students, "It took the paramedics thirty minutes to get there. What do you fear for Barbara?"

My students, now sitting on the edges of their seats fully engaged and focused, uttered sadly, "Barbara must be dead."

"Why would Barbara have died?" I asked.

"Because she would have bled to death from being stabbed," several students answered.

I continued. When the police and paramedics came I took them back to where I last saw her. She was gone. All the police could see in the beam of their flashlights was blood. Suddenly a porch light went out across the street, we heard a door slamming on a car, followed by the shrieks of tires as it sped away. The police officers began running over towards the house shining their flash lights everywhere. And there, lying on the porch, was Barbara. She had apparently crawled up on the porch looking for help.

Now my students cannot hold back. They start asking almost in unison, "Was Barbara dead? Did she die?"

Not only was Barbara alive, she began swearing at the police for shining the light in her eyes and yelling at the paramedics who were feverishly trying to stop the flow of blood from her gaping wounds.

"Why didn't Barbara bleed to death?" I asked.

The students immediately started yelling out, "It was because of the drugs Barbara took, the barbiturates!"

"And what do you think the drugs did?"

"The drugs must have slowed her heart down"

"Exactly right! So why wasn't Barbara screaming out in pain?"

Now confident of their answers, they shouted, "Because the barbiturates must stop pain!"

"You are right again!"

I then conducted a short impromptu quiz, "Amphetamines decrease the heart rate, true or false?"

"False!" the students yelled out.

"Barbiturates increase a persons ability to endure pain!"

"True!" they shouted.

After about a dozen or so questions, all of which the students knew the answers to, it was time to complete class. Before they left I ended the story by sharing that while Barbara survived the ordeal she remained in a wheel chair for the rest of her life.

"So, you will never forget what barbiturates do to the body because you will never forget whom?"

And my students, along with my guests, answered, "Barbara."

After dismissing my eager to learn and enthusiastic sixth graders, I explained to my guests that this lesson was an example of how to teach children using 'symbolic imagery.' I shared with them that had I begun this class with the typical format of handing out a paper with a picture of an amphetamine and a barbiturate on it which described the various properties of each of the drugs, together with a list of study questions at the end, that piece of paper would have more likely been used as a paper airplane than a study guide. However, if I brought that same paper in tomorrow my students will respond enthusiastically because the contents of the paper will have value and meaning to them.

Treating relationships as preeminent; attuning ourselves to temporal rhythms; emphasizing learning through subjective barometers and symbolic imagery: These are at the core of African American culture. We feel them, know them to be true. Our mission is to integrate them and learn how to use them to our advantage in the world in which we find ourselves.

It is not surprising that a culture that places primary concern in people's relationship with each other would evolve learning strategies that place great emphasis on internal orientations and symbolic imagery, especially when it comes to interactions with other people. To be sure, both subjective and objective strategies are important if we are to fully understand our world. Difficulties can arise however, when objective means are used as the primary method of understanding people or when more internal means are similarly applied to working with the material world.

When a culture becomes overly concerned with their relationship to the material world, even people can become objectified. Individuals can grow to be viewed as cogs in a great machine and, as such, expendable. In extreme cases this can lead to horrific results, such as when accountants at Ford Motor Company recommended that Ford not recall and repair the faulty gas tanks in one of their cars, the Ford Pinto, and one of their light trucks. These accountants concluded that it would cost less to pay off the lawsuits resulting from death and injury than it would cost to fix the problem. Ford's executives followed their recommendation. In 1977, Mark Dowie, writing for "Mother Jone's Magazine," broke the story. In his article he released the following internal memorandum from Ford depicting the math they used to make their case.

Benefits and Costs Relating to Fuel Leakage Associated with the Static Rollover Test Portion of FMVSS208. [4]

From Ford Motor Company internal memorandum: "Fatalities Associated with Crash-Induced Fuel Leakage and Fires.":

BENEFITS

Savings: 180 burn deaths, 180 serious burn injuries, 2,100 burned vehicles.

Unit Cost: $200,000 per death, $67,000 per injury, $700 per vehicle.

Total Benefit: 180 X ($200,000) + 180 X ($67,000) + $2,100 X ($700) = **$49.5 million.**

COSTS

Sales: 11 million cars, 1.5 million light trucks.

Unit Cost: $11 per car, $11 per truck.

Total Cost: 11,000,000 X ($11) + 1,500,000 X ($11) = **$137 million.**

Ford concluded it would cost $49.5 million to pay the victims of the burn deaths and injuries that would likely occur as a result of not fixing their design flaw, considerably less than the $137 million it would have cost them to fix the flaw. This would save Ford $87.5 million.

Though this actuarial analysis was correct, mathematically speaking, it proved to be incomplete and quite shortsighted. It failed to take into account the positive effect recalling and repairing their cars would have on the Ford automobile owners and potential buyers. In addition to saving lives, recalling and repairing their cars would certainly have added to the public's respect for and confidence in Ford Motor Company. Of course, factors like consumer respect and confidence, though no less important (and perhaps more so) than dollars and cents, are more difficult to reduce to numbers. As it was, when Ford's actions were brought to light, they eventually had to fix their mistakes and ended up looking very bad in the process.

In the grand scheme of things Ford's actions might seem relatively inconsequential, except to those who were needlessly burned or killed in one of their cars. When material gain becomes the god before which all must be sacrificed, even one's own humanity, all manner of crimes and pursuant justifications become possible. And when crimes become heinous enough, as in wars of aggression, genocide and enslavement, the perpetrators have little choice but to dehumanize their victims.

Chapter 2:

Whole to Three-Fifths:

Dehumanization

And Miriam and Aaron spake against Moses because of the Ethiopian woman whom he had married: for he had married an Ethiopian woman.

. . . And the anger of the Lord was kindled against them

Numbers 12: 1-9

When I bring up the issue of slavery, all too often I am met with these words: "C'mon now, slavery was an accepted institution throughout the world for thousands of years. Every culture has had slaves. Americans were no different." I cannot begin to tell you how many times white people have presented this argument to me. Perhaps this is just another effort to trivialize or justify America's crime. Perhaps its just another way people try to resolve their internal conflicts. Whatever the motivation, the lengths people will go **not** to confront their own history has never ceased to amaze me.

The truth is American chattel slavery was very different from most varieties of enslavement that preceded it. It differed in the manner in which a person became a slave; it differed in the treatment of slaves; it differed in the length of servitude; most of all, it differed in the way owners viewed their slaves.

Before the European slave trade began in 1440, most people who became slaves became so as the result of war. Two societies went to war and the winners enslaved the losers. Sometimes, as was the case with Rome, a dominant society would need more laborers, so they made war on a weaker state and took the manpower they required. Europeans, however, systematically turned the capturing, shipping and selling of other human beings into a business, a business that would develop into the backbone of an entire economy, providing the foundation for the world's wealthiest nation. The first slaves arrived in the Americas from Africa in the early 1500's. The transatlantic slave trade was made illegal in the United States in 1808 and continued in other parts of the Americas until 1870. Estimates of the number of people captured and transported during those 430 years vary. Reasonable estimates place the figure between 20 and 30 million.

Slavery is a brutal institution in any society, yet it seems the treatment of slaves by Europeans was particularly so. In ancient Greece, Rome and throughout the African continent, though slaves were considered to be the property of their slave masters, they often had legal status. Many were able to ultimately gain freedom and citizenship. Slaves were granted freedom under a number of circumstances depending upon the role in which they served. Masters frequently liberated slaves that were considered faithful and loyal. Many slaves over time purchased their freedom. It was not uncommon for owners to free females for the purposes of marriage, in which case children from these marriages were usually free.

During the time of American chattel slavery it was exceedingly rare for a slave to be freed and rarer still for a slave to buy his or her freedom. Though slave owners fathered many children by their female slaves they never married them, and the overwhelming majority of the children they fathered remained enslaved throughout their lifetimes. Even if they wanted to marry it was illegal to do so. While many societies educated their slaves, southern colonies and later states, usually outlawed such practices. In most societies it was extremely rare for a slave population to reproduce itself through breeding, as did American slaves. Typically, children born to slaves in places other than the Americas were born free. In many societies slavery was more akin to indentured servitude. There was a fixed amount of time a slave was held in service to his owner, after such time he would be granted his or her freedom. In America, generations were born into slavery and died there.

That black Africans sold other black Africans into slavery is well known and is often offered as a rationalization by apologists for the institution of slavery. This has lead to significant misunderstandings regarding the role of Africans in the slave trade. When enemy tribes in Africa made war, the conqueror took prisoners and made them what we call indentured servants, not chattel. With the coming of the European slavers, vanquished warriors could be sold in an effort to reduce the 'enemy' tribe's warrior forces. Even so, Africans could not imagine the level of degradation and hardship experienced by slaves in the Americas since they did not behave that way toward those they conquered. Consequently, when Africans sold their captives to white slave merchants, there was no way for them to know how they were to be treated upon their arrival in America. There is no way to determine how Africans would have responded had they been aware of the conditions to which they were condemning those they sold.

Of greatest import, the American slavery experience was exclusively based on the notion of racial inferiority. According to Thomas D. Morris in his book, *Southern Slavery and the Law, 1619 – 1860*, Africans were considered to be 'presumed' or 'natural slaves' based on their skin color. They were also referred to as 'thinking property' and inherently 'rightless persons.'[5] In few societies, if any, were so large a group of people considered to be less than human based upon physical appearance. Yet Europeans concluded that black Africans were fitted by a natural act of God to the position of permanent bondage. It was this relegation to lesser humanity that allowed the institution of chattel slavery to be intrinsically linked with violence, and it was through violence, aggression and dehumanization that the institution of slavery was enacted, legislated and perpetuated by Europeans.

The Three-Fifths Compromise

"We subscribe to the doctrine," might one of our Southern brethren observe, ``that representation relates more immediately to persons, and taxation more immediately to property, and we join in the application of this distinction to the case of our slaves. But we must deny the fact, that slaves are considered merely as property, and in no respect whatever as persons. The true state of the case is, that they partake of both these qualities: being considered by our laws, in some respects, as persons, and in other respects as property. In being compelled to labor, not for himself, but for a master; in being vendible by one master to another master; and in being subject at all times to be restrained in his liberty and chastised in his body, by the capricious will of another, the slave may appear to be degraded from the human rank, and classed with those irrational animals which fall under the legal denomination of property. In being protected, on the other hand, in his life and in his limbs, against the violence of all others, even the master of his labor and his liberty; and in being punishable himself for all violence committed against others, the slave is no less evidently regarded by the law as a member of the society, not as a part of the irrational creation; as a moral person, not as a mere article of property. The federal Constitution, therefore, decides with great propriety on the case of our slaves, when it views them in the mixed character of

*persons and of property. This is in fact their true character. It is the
character bestowed on them by the laws under which they live; and it will
not be denied, that these are the proper criterion; because it is only under
the pretext that the laws have transformed the Negroes into subjects of
property, that a place is disputed them in the computation of numbers;
and it is admitted, that if the laws were to restore the rights which have
been taken away, the Negroes could no longer be refused an equal share
of representation with the other inhabitants."* [6]

Sound confusing? It should. Let me put this passage in perspective.
James Madison (the primary author of our Constitution and a slave
holder) wrote this passage during the Constitutional Convention of 1787.
One of the most heated debates at the convention was what to do about
the slaves. A number of delegates from Northern States saw this as an
opportunity to abolish slavery. Most of the southern delegates (most of
whom were slave owners) intended to continue the practice. After much

heated argument and debate all but one state agreed
to eliminate slavery.

That one state, South Carolina, threatened to go its
own way and not become part of the United States if
slavery was to be curtailed. The delegates, unwilling
to lose South Carolina, acceded to its demands and so
were stalemated. To resolve this logjam the delegates
decided to table the discussion of abolition to a later
date. Slavery would continue to be legal under the Constitution.

This posed another problem: How were slaves to be figured into each
state's population count?   Delegates considered this: the more people
residing in a state, the more representatives that particular state can send
to the House of Representatives, and hence the more power that state can
wield. Northern delegates, arguing that since slaveholders view slaves as
property and grant them no rights, proposed that slaves not be counted

at all towards a state's total population. Southern delegates attempted to argue that slaves should be counted as part of the population.

The quote above is an example of an attempt at resolving the problem. The main thrust of Madison's argument is that slaves should be considered property for tax purposes and individuals for the purpose of determining a state's population. He goes on to explain how it is that slaves are both persons and property. You can see the absurdity of his argument and the ludicrousness of the situation. Here you have slave owners, having just defended their view that slaves are property, in part as justification for committing some of the most heinous crimes against other human beings, now trying to claim them as persons. And why? So they can have greater power in the soon-to-be-formed federal government. Why did they need this power? To continue the institution of slavery as the economic juggernaut it had become and to prevent the Northerners from passing legislation for its dismantling.

The agreed upon solution to this problem was the "Three-Fifths Compromise." Rather than each slave being counted as a person, three-fifths of a state's slave population would be counted toward that state's total population. In this way slaves became three-fifths of a human.

Cognitive Dissonance: Easing the Conscience

By the time of Madison it was generally accepted among many people in America that blacks were inferior. A significant portion of the population viewed Africans as a lesser species of human than those of European descent. Native Americans fell into the same sub-class of human. Why did these views come to be so widely held? Why did the humanity of Africans as well as Native Americans come into question?

When we commit a negative act or think about doing so most of us get uncomfortable. This discomfort is caused by the difference between our action and what we believe about ourselves. For example, most of us would experience a certain amount of discomfort if we were to seriously consider robbing someone and even greater discomfort if we were to actually do it. Why? Because most of us think of ourselves as decent people and decent people do not rob others. This discomfort is called "Cognitive Dissonance." Cognitive - having to do with thinking: Dissonance - meaning discord. The greater the difference between our actions and what we think about ourselves, the greater the cognitive dissonance and so, our discomfort.

Humans do not particularly like this discomfort so whenever it occurs we almost immediately try to resolve it. And we can resolve it one of two ways. One way is to own up to the negative act and address the harm caused by it. The other way is to justify the negative act rather than admit any wrongdoing. "They deserved it," is a typical justification. In instances of particularly egregious negative acts like wars of aggression, enslavement and genocide the perpetrators have to go so far as to demonize and in the many cases, dehumanize their victims.

During the past 500 years Europeans have spent significant resources to 'prove' Africans and those of African descent are inferior. The difference between the actions of the Europeans (i.e., enslaving, raping, and killing) and their beliefs about themselves (i.e., 'We are good Christians') was so great and the cognitive dissonance so painful, that they were obliged to go to great lengths in order to survive their own horrific behavior. Chattel slavery and genocide of the Native American population were so un-Christian the only way they could make their actions acceptable, and so resolve the dissonance, was to relegate their victims to the level of sub-human. Madison's statement earlier in this chapter serves to demonstrate how far intelligent men will go in their efforts to rationalize their untenable positions.

Europe's efforts to justify slavery and the slave trade began in the 16th century and America followed suit soon after. In her book, *A New History of Social Welfare*, Phyllis Day observes,

Virginia led the way in enslavement of people of African heritage
when in 1660 it made them servants for life, forbade intermarriage with
whites, and gave children born of African-descended women the status of
their mothers. Although there were some religious qualms about making
Christians slaves, in 1667 it was decreed that conversion to Christianity
would have no bearing on slave status.

Slavery as practiced in North America was a response to the
Protestant religioeconomic dictum that wealth demonstrates morality
and to the even older dictum of fear and hatred of "outsiders." Because
Africans did not worship the Christian God, their lives were insignificant
compared to the mandate of wealth for their masters.

. . . Slavery was not for the most part seen as evil at all but almost a
morality, since it "protected" slaves from destitution, put them to work,
and led to wealth for God's chosen. These beliefs created a system of
slavery unequaled in brutality and gave rise to the American brand of
racism. [7]

Being a Virginian, Madison came from a hundred and forty year
tradition of resolving cognitive dissonance by dehumanizing those
of African descent. By the time the Constitutional Convention was
complete Madison and the other founding fathers determined Africans
were equivalent to three-fifths of a human. It didn't end there. Efforts
to prove blacks inferior continue to this day. These efforts have been so
successful that many white people believe their superiority to be true and
many others, while they don't believe it, will act like they do. Even more
telling, many African Americans act like they believe it as well.

The Power of Definition

Most of us have found ourselves deeply engrossed in a conversation
with friends or peers where someone tries, to no avail, to convince the
group that his or her view is correct and true. Two common strategies

are employed in order to convince the errant disbelievers. The first is to state that the point being presented can be substantiated as true because it can be found in a 'book,' and as such, confirms their position to be 'the truth.' The second strategy is to state that which is being espoused has been 'scientifically proven.' What we often believe to be 'scientific fact' is no more than a strongly held, unsubstantiated belief. Hence not all that is written in a book or touted to be science can be accepted as truth.

How did we get here? To fully appreciate the depths of the misconceptions, misunderstandings and outright lies that underpinned the dehumanization of Africans and their descendents, we first need to be clear about some basic concepts and how they relate to each other. The following definitions are taken from *Webster's Dictionary*:

Opinion: *1. A belief or judgment based on grounds insufficient to produce complete certainty. 2. A personal view, attitude or appraisal.*

Belief: *1. Something believed; opinion; conviction.*
2. Confidence in the truth or existence of something not immediately susceptible to rigorous proof.

Fact: *1. Something that actually exists. 2. Something known to exist or to have happened. 3. A truth known by actual experience or observation; something known to be true.*

Truth: *1. The true or actual state of a matter. 3. A verified or indisputable fact, proposition, principle or the like.*

Science: *1. A branch of knowledge or study dealing with a body of facts or truths about the physical or material world gained through observation and experimentation.*

Theory: *A proposed explanation whose status is still conjectural.*[8]

So an opinion is basically a thought about the world and a belief is an opinion about the world that we have confidence in and/or hold with strong conviction. We all have opinions and beliefs. We have opinions and beliefs about politics, entertainment, sports, and the people in our families. It is important to note that neither opinions nor beliefs necessarily have a basis in fact or truth. Believing something to be true has no impact on its verity. Believing in Santa Claus really, really hard will not increase the chances of a big guy in a red suit riding across the sky on a sled driven by reindeer the night before Christmas. Be this as it may, beliefs are important. Some of our beliefs serve us well; others can be disadvantageous.

Facts are pieces of information about something that actually happened and/or actually exists. What we think about these facts are our opinions or beliefs. "Abraham Lincoln was the sixteenth president of the United States." Fact. "Lincoln was a great president." Opinion or belief. "The sun rises in the east." Fact. "The sun is beautiful." Opinion. Compared to beliefs and opinions, facts are relatively rare. Believing things to be facts does not make them so. For centuries European scholars believed the earth was flat and the sun revolved around it. They were wrong on both counts.

Where facts are pieces of information, truth is the whole story. Facts can be used to mislead as well as to enlighten. The best liars use facts to perpetrate their deceptions.

"Did you sleep with her?" asks the parent.

"No, I did not 'sleep' with her," replies the son.

The fact is they did not sleep together. The truth is they had sex. You know the difference. The truth often is only revealed when you have all the facts.

Science is an approach to gaining knowledge. Science uses known facts and truths to develop a greater understanding about ourselves and our world. Opinions and beliefs have little place in science. Most good science is advanced through observation and rigorous experimentation.

At times a scientist may have an intuitive insight into the nature of the world. Then, using the scientific method, he or she would test that insight. Sometimes they leave the testing to others. However, until that insight is tested it remains theoretical and cannot be assumed to be true.

A theory simply is a proposed explanation about the world. More simply, a theory is a guess. A good theory is a thoughtfully considered, very well-educated series of suppositions. Such a series of suppositions remains a theory until it has been fully tested and proven correct. We still call it Darwin's theory of evolution. There is still too much about evolution we do not know. Post Traumatic Slave Syndrome falls in this category. It is a theory meant to explain how and why we move the way we do in the world.

So, those are some concepts we must be clear about. As you will see, all manner of opinions, beliefs, half truths and outright lies have been presented over the years to 'prove' blacks are inferior to whites. Many of these were presented in the name of science, and many of these were printed in textbooks, scientific journals and media of the era. The effort to prove white superiority goes on to this very day and it is important for us to be able to differentiate fact from fiction.

Science and Fiction

Cognitive dissonance may be one of the answers to the question, 'Why did Europeans need to view blacks as sub-human?' Next we must explore, 'How did Europeans convince themselves those of African descent were a lesser class of human?'

18th Century Rationale

The answer begins with the preeminent biological scientist of the 18th century, Carl Von Linnaeus (1707-1778). Some of you may remember him from your high school or college biology class. He was responsible for the taxonomic system we use today to classify life: kingdom, phylum, class, order, family, genus, species. Using his system we are able to know every living thing's relation to all other living things.

Thanks to Linnaeus we can know the place of each kind of plant and animal we find on earth. Cows and oxen are bovines. Douglas firs, giant sequoias and redwoods are all conifers. Panthers, tigers, jaguars and leopards are all felines. All bovines and felines are mammals. He delineated the characteristics that made each life form fall into each group. His system was based totally on observations of an organism's physical looks. It was a truly impressive and valuable achievement.

The problem was he went too far. He expanded his system to try to account for different 'types' of humans, and unlike all his previous work he classified humans using considerably fewer objective descriptors. With this highly suspect effort to classify humans, Linnaeus began the science of anthropology and laid the foundation for 19th century beliefs about race that resulted in racism. In his work, *Systema Naturae*, he set forth his race classification system using color as a criterion for classifying races, while also assigning moral and intellectual capacities to each race. These concepts became a permanent part of 19th century anthropological thought and language. According to Haller, in his book *Outcasts From Evolution,*

Linnaeus describes Homo Americanus as reddish, choleric, obstinate, contented, and regulated by custom; Homo Europaeus as white, fickle, sanguine, blue-eyed, gentle and governed by laws; Homo Asiaticus as sallow, grave dignified, avaricious, and ruled by opinion; and Homo Afer as black, phlegmatic, cunning, lazy, lustful, careless, and governed by caprice. [9]

Of course it is not hard to figure out whom he is describing. Now, lets go back to our definitions. Linnaeus was a preeminent scientist. Did any of these descriptions have anything to do with science? Were any experiments designed to see if his observations were correct? Did he even have any intention to design experiments to test them? Do any of them have any basis in fact or truth? The answers to all of these questions is a resounding NO!!

So Linnaeus was just expressing his opinions. Maybe he actually believed what he wrote, yet we know belief does not make a thing true. None of his observations, other than perhaps humans have different skin pigmentation, have any basis in fact or truth. They really cannot even be considered so much as a theory. The trouble was he wrote them in his book as if they were facts and truths and others believed him.

Linnaeus' misguided opinions provided the backdrop for other researchers to develop their theories of race classification. Johann Friedrich Blumenbach (1752-1840), in his treatise *On The Natural Variety of Mankind*, developed his own system of classification, grouping man into the categories of Caucasian, Mongolian, American, Ethiopian, and Malayan races. As Haller relates,

> *While Linnaeus founded his classificatory system principally upon skin color, Blumenbach considered a combination of color, hair, skull, and facial characteristics as a fundamental means for classifying the five varieties of man. Central to his study was the Caucasian, a term which he originated. He took the name from Mount Caucasus because its southern slope cradled what he felt to be the most beautiful race of men; the Georgian. The Caucasus, near Mount Ararat, upon which the biblical ark came to rest after the flood, seemed the most appropriate source for the original race of man.* [10]

Haller goes on to quote Blumenbach,

> *For, in the first place, the stock displays, as we have seen, the most beautiful form of the skull, from which, as a mean and primeval type,*

the others diverge by most easy gradations on both sides to the two ultimate extremes (that is, on the one side the Mongolian, on the other the Ethiopian). Besides, it is white in color, which we may fairly assume to have been the primitive color of mankind . . . [11]

Let's see . . . skull bones being white lead him to the conclusion that Europeans were the first humans? Blumenbach was also a 'scientist.' Did any of these descriptions have anything to do with science? Were any experiments designed to see if his observations were correct? Did he even have any intention to design experiments to test them? Do any of them have any basis in fact or truth? The answers to all these questions again is a resounding NO!!

So Blumenbach was also just expressing his opinions. Perhaps he also actually believed what he wrote, but like Linnaeus, none of his observations had any basis in fact, nor do they meet the standard for being considered a theory. The trouble was he, like his predecessor, wrote them as if they were facts and truths, and those who needed to assuage their guilt took his and Linnaeus' work as gospel.

Despite the fact that both Linnaeus and Blumenbach had failed to produce a shred of scientific evidence to support their opinions, their ideas continued to be referenced in scientific communities throughout the western world. Given the widespread dissemination of these fallacious beliefs, it is not difficult to understand why belief in racial superiority took root in the 18th century and continues to exist today.

Africans were among the many civilizations around the world who did not live up to European standards and so were considered inferior. They were inferior, first because they were not European, and second because they were not Christian. Thus, Africans were viewed as impure, irreligious and uncivilized, fit to be slaves.

In America, these efforts to 'prove' whites superior to blacks continued in the grand European tradition. Thomas Jefferson, considered one of the most learned men of his era, expressed disdain and contempt for blacks, stating that:

> *They smelled bad and were physically unattractive, required less sleep, were dumb, cowardly and incapable of feeling grief.*

In his attempt to justify slavery he went on to write:

> *. . . It is not against experience to suppose, that different species of the same genus, or varieties of the same species, may possess different qualifications. Will not a lover of natural history then, one who views the gradations in all the races of animals with the eye of philosophy, excuse an effort to keep those in the department of man as distinct as nature has formed them? This unfortunate difference of colour, and perhaps of faculty, is a powerful obstacle to the emancipation of these people."*

Finally concluding:

> *. . . advance it therefore as a suspicion only, that blacks, whether originally a distinct race, or made distinct by time and circumstances, are inferior to the whites in the endowments of body and mind.* [12]

Contrary to his doubts Jefferson's feelings on this matter were so strong that he suggested that blacks be removed from any possible contact with whites lest the race be tainted.

> *Among the Romans emancipation required but one effort. The slave, when made free, might mix with, without staining the blood of the master. But with us a second is necessary, unknown to history. When freed, he is to be removed beyond the reach of mixture.* [13]

Other founding fathers expressed similar views as to the status of blacks. James Madison, framer of our Constitution, viewed slaves as,

> . . . *inhabitants, but as debased by servitude below the equal level of free inhabitants; which regards the* slave *as divested of two-fifths of the* man. [14]

Further efforts to dehumanize those brought here from Africa were written into law. The Virginia Code of 1705 removed criminal consequences for killing a slave in the act of correcting them:

> *And if any slave resist his master, or owner, or other person, by his or her order, correcting such slave, and shall happen to be killed in such correction, it shall not be accounted a felony; but the master, owner and every such other person so giving correction, shall be free and acquit of all punishment and accusation for the same, as if such accident had never happened.* [15]

A similar bill enacted in Jackson, Mississippi, remained on the books until 1985 when, much to the embarrassment of the Mississippi Legislature, it was discovered and voted out. The Virginia code also referred to as the *"Casual Killing Act,"* demonstrated that slaves lacked even the most basic protection under the law, the right of self-preservation.

And the efforts to 'prove' superiority continued. Slavery produced or supported a white ethnocentric model, which was justified by an erroneous belief in 'colorism,' the legal assumption that a colored person is a slave. Life was viewed as being part of a chain that ascended from the lowest to the highest order. Such an analysis, together with the Aristotelian notion of the natural slave and finally the perversion of the so-called "curse of Ham" in Christianity, raised and answered the crucial question for southern whites, at least by the nineteenth century: which 'race' of people were natural slaves? This point of view further cemented white supremacy as the desired model and the culture of African Americans as the subhuman underclass. In 1858 *An Inquiry into the Law of Negro Slavery in the United States of America*, T. R. R. Cobb asserted,

> *This inquiry into the physical, mental, and moral development of the Negro race seems to point them clearly, as peculiarly fitted for a laborious class. Their physical frame is capable of great and long exertion. Their mental capacity renders them incapable of successful self-development, and yet adapts them for the direction of wiser race. Their moral character renders them happy, peaceful, contented, and cheerful in a status that would break the spirit and destroy the energies of the Caucasian or the native American.* [16]

Phrenology

By the mid-1800's, the effort to 'scientifically prove' white superiority had support from another front, the 'science' of phrenology. Phrenology's adherents claimed you could discover much about a person by examining his or her skull. Phrenologists believed the bumps on the skull coincided with brain development and so through careful examination one could draw conclusions about an individual's intellect and personality. As you might imagine, some of these 'scientists' used this discipline to classify groups of people in order of intelligence. For instance, in 1859 the noted phrenologists O.L. and L.N. Fowler in their book, *The Self-Instructor in Phrenology and Physiology*, wrote,

The various races also accord with phrenological science. Thus, Africans generally have full perceptives, and large Tuner and Language, but retiring Causality, and accordingly are deficient in reasoning capacity, yet have excellent memories and lingual and musical powers.

Indians possess extraordinary strength of the propensities and perceptives, yet have no great moral or inventive power: and, hence, have very wide, round, conical, and rather low heads, but are large over the eyes . . .

. . . Finally, contrast the massive foreheads all giant-minded men – Bacons, Franklins, Miltons, etc. with the low retiring foreheads of idiots. In short, every human, every brutal head, is constructed throughout strictly on phrenological principles. Ransack air earth and water and not one palpable exception ever has been, ever can be adduced. This wholesale view of this science precludes the possibility of mistake. Phrenology is therefore a part and parcel of nature – a universal fact.[17]

Was phrenology science? Of course not. Unlike the works of Linnaeus and Blumenbach, at least Phrenology achieved the status of theory. From the time of its first postulation around 1790 in Vienna through the time of its final debunking in the 1890's, phrenology was proven inadequate again and again. Systematic research validating its predictions were never performed, yet phrenology was still accepted as 'scientific' evidence as to the superiority of whites and inferiority of blacks by those looking for such rationalizations. Actually, a number of European anthropologists used it to claim European superiority over **all** other peoples on the planet. Not surprisingly, phrenology originated in Europe and was in vogue throughout the United States.

The Fallacy of Intelligence Testing

Linnaeus, Blumenbach, the Founding Fathers, Phrenology. The effort continued in the United States throughout the 20th century with intelligence or IQ testing. Yes, intelligence testing originated in our country. At various times in this century it was big business. In the 50's, 60's, and 70's 'What's your IQ?' was a very popular question. Some industries used IQ's to evaluate prospective employees. School systems used IQ's to track students along academic and vocational paths. IQ's were a very big deal. We are still testing people today. In fact, some researchers still use such testing as an effort to 'prove' the superiority of one group of people over another. The amazing thing about all this testing is that IQ's are meaningless numbers, scientifically speaking.

In his book *The Mismeasure of Man*, Stephen J. Gould reviews the history of intelligence testing and discusses its problems. His work is quite fascinating and I highly recommend reading it. It is important to understand Gould's work because IQ testing is widely accepted as science, just as Linnaeus' work was accepted as such in his day, and we must understand how little science was actually involved in its development. Intelligence testing is more or less the 20th Century's version of Phrenology.

It all started with Alfred Binet, an educator at the turn of the century in France. He noticed a few of his students would fall behind and wondered if he could create a test that would help him identify these students so he could give them more attention sooner. In his writings he specifically cautioned readers not to think of his test as having anything to do with intelligence; intelligence being, he believed, inherently unmeasurable.

In the early 1900's, a group of American social scientists disregarded Binet's warning, began modifying his test and eventually concocted tests they simply asserted measured intelligence. The end result of these concoctions was the Stanford-Binet Intelligence Test, the granddaddy of all IQ tests, the test all other IQ tests have been measured against for decades.

Among the first people to be tested were Polish, Russian, Italian and other Southern and Eastern European immigrants just getting off boats at Ellis Island. You can imagine what it must have been like for these people. They had just spent days cramped in the hold of the ship. They were tired, hungry, feeling the stress of arriving in a new country, hopeful, yet not certain how they will survive. Most, of course, did not speak English. They got off the ship and were herded towards a building where they were poked, prodded and examined. In the midst of these medical examinations they were given a test in a foreign language to measure their 'intelligence.' How do you think they did? Needless to say, they did rather poorly. After tabulating the results, the 'scientists' concluded that Poland, Russia, Italy and other countries were sending us their least intelligent citizens, their dregs.

Did the Stanford-Binet Intelligence Test actually measure intelligence? Almost certainly not. We cannot know for sure because the test was never validated. When we say a test is valid we mean that the test, in fact, measures what the authors say its supposed to measure. In order to validate a test one must compare the results of the test with actual, objective outcomes in the real world. And herein lies the problem: because there is no objective way to measure intelligence in the first place, it is impossible to ever validate such a test.

So, even though the Stanford-Binet Intelligence Test was never proved to be valid, its proponents continued to assert they had a test of intelligence. They made such a good case, pseudo-scientific though it was, that America started buying into the concept of measuring intelligence. Since then, many different intelligence tests have been designed. The trouble remains, we cannot know what any of these tests actually measure. [18]

So far, no intelligence test has ever been proven to measure intelligence. More importantly, these tests have little to no predictive value. They cannot accurately predict whether a person will be successful. They cannot accurately predict how much effort a person will put into living their life. They cannot even accurately predict how well a person will do in school. Yet for the better part of the last hundred years or so there have been those who have used intelligence testing as a means to validate their superiority.

One more thing about intelligence testing: A lot of attention has been placed on the test questions themselves being culturally biased and there is certainly evidence of that. However, more to the point is that these tests, culturally biased or not, do not measure anything substantial. Why we persist in using them is much more a testament to good marketing than to good science.

Linneaus' taxonomy, Jeffersonian reasoning, Phrenology, and IQ testing all served as the 'scientific' foundations upon which the institutions of slavery and racial superiority/inferiority were constructed. Since the time the first slaves arrived in the Americas from Africa in the early 1500's to present day, Europeans and their descendents have gone to great lengths to justify the 500 years of trauma and dehumanization they and their institutions produced. The effects of this trauma and dehumanization are observable today, and can be explained by the theory of Post Traumatic Slave Syndrome.

Chapter 3:

Crimes Against Humanity

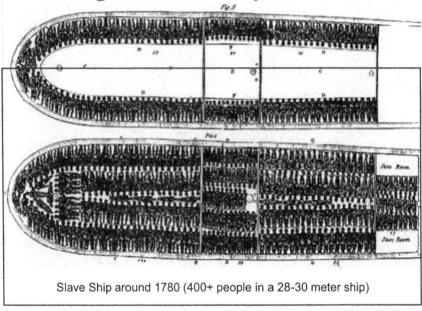

Slave Ship around 1780 (400+ people in a 28-30 meter ship)

In the fall of 2004, on one of my visits to New York City, I was asked to speak to a group of 16 to 18 year old incarcerated young men. Though I had often spoken to young prisoners, I was not prepared for what awaited me this time in New York. I was going to Riker's Island.

We were driven to a set of bungalows, the last stop before crossing the bridge to the prison. I watched as hundreds of cars traveled to and fro across the bridge, unaware that it led exclusively to the island of prisoners. The traffic was not different from any of the bridges I had traveled during my visits to New York over the years: nonstop movement, endless wayfarers bound to various destinations (albeit less restrictive than Rikers, but oftentimes no less dismal – one has only to look at the city's poorest neighborhoods).

As we made our way over the bridge I cannot describe the awesome feeling of dread that began to shroud my emotions. A sea of barbed wire with razor sharp edges resembling the ominous rows of teeth of a great white shark stretched as far as my eyes could take in. But the predators that inhabited this island did not live in the turbulent waters which encircled what I was told was the largest penal institution in the world. These predators wore the drab uniforms of captives and the no less dreary garb of armed prison guards. The guards had the added wardrobe accessory of weapons that seemed to come in all sizes and shapes. The only color that I can recall from my visit is gray. This gray color covered more than the buildings and the uniforms of this massive prison, it seemed to engulf the spirits of its inhabitants.

As we drove I asked one of my escorts, a school administrator, about the demographics of the prison.

"The prison has roughly 15,000 employees, with 14,000 inmates made up of men, women and youth," he said matter-of-factly.

I was stunned but managed to ask a second question, "What is the racial or ethnic make-up of the inmate population?"

This resulted in an even more devastating reply. He hesitated a bit before answering, as if he bore some personal shame associated with his response. "The inmate population is eighty-five percent African American."

I was so staggered I didn't even hear who comprised the remaining fifteen percent. I became numb, hearing only my own heart beating in my ears. I wondered how many Americans were aware of this island penitentiary that housed multitudes of nameless black people. And if people were aware, why was there no public outrage? Here the word 'overrepresentation' is the grossest of understatements that fails to account for so blatant a wrong. Yet, this unspeakable crime has been committed in the plain sight of us all and required our collective will in order to be perpetrated. I thought if Americans could ignore a tenth of Rwanda's inhabitants being slaughtered and millions of others dislocated, why should these thousands of black men, women and youths warrant any American's notice? After all, they're criminals and we are just protecting the 'common good.'

When we arrived at our destination I was taken to a large room, which they referred to as the chapel, though it lacked any similarity to a traditional religious hall except for the rows of pews. There, 150 young men were seated, neatly separated into four sections with armed guards surrounding the room. I stood on a slightly raised platform with a large podium. Consistent with the prison's demographics, I looked out into a sea of nearly all black faces.

I began by telling them who I was and why I was there. I shared that one of my missions was to help prevent young African American males from ever entering correctional institutions. I went on to say that another of my desires was to ensure that those in the audience would never return to Rikers. Mostly I talked about Post Traumatic Slave Syndrome and how young men were being socialized in prisons, and like homing pigeons, being conditioned to return. At first I sensed they didn't believe I really wanted to talk to *them*. By the end of the presentation, though, the youths were asking questions and sharing their experiences.

My husband and I stayed briefly to talk to one group of the young prisoners. My husband explained what they would face upon their release and encouraged them, telling them how to create their own businesses rather than hoping for a job. They continued to yell out questions as they were being escorted out of the chapel and they reached out to shake our hands. They had entered the room as prisoners, but they left the room as hopeful young black youth, not unlike our own sons.

News about the session apparently spread quickly and by the time I was ready to leave, the island staff, many of whom had been at the prison for over 15 years, told me they had never seen such a positive response from that population. I would love to believe that my husband and I had done something earth-shaking or brilliantly unique to engender such a favorable response from the young men. In reality, the only thing we had consciously done was 'respect' them. That was apparently enough.

Un-sanitizing American History

Studying history in American schools we learn about the excesses of the Roman Empire, the viciousness of Stalin's Soviet Union and the brutality of the Nazis. We learn about the barbarity of the Mongols and the cruelty of the Huns. You can easily add to this list the Japanese during World War II, the Viet Cong and the Huutu Nation. Currently we have Milosevic's Serbia, Hussein's Iraq, the Taliban, and Osama bin Laden, to name but a few.

Certainly all of those listed above are responsible for their fair share of atrocities. But missing from this list is one society that is responsible for some of the most gruesome crimes against humanity in history – The United States of America. While the powers that be in America are happy to talk about others' crimes, they seem to be reluctant to truly confront their own. With respect to the genocide of Native Americans, and the enslavement and later oppression of those of African descent, the history we in this land learn has been greatly sanitized.

In many regards this was the hardest chapter of the book to write. For weeks on end my research took me to narratives, stories and reports that knotted my stomach, moved me to rage and brought me to tears. How do I make real the pain and suffering of our ancestors? How do I give their experiences appropriate recognition? How do I bring to people's awareness the vileness of those that perpetrated these crimes?

In some ways this can never be done because we have trouble

confronting such pain and suffering. We really don't want to put ourselves in their place. For most of us it's just too hard. Even many of the accounts written by those who lived through these times are strangely absent of emotion, as if no words could communicate their experience.

Have you ever had a really severe migraine headache? Have you ever had a terrible case of the flu? Have you had to battle cancer? Have you ever been in a car accident, or injured yourself so badly, where the pain was so intense and persistent, that all you wanted was medication to knock yourself out? In these moments the pain and misery consumes you. It's all you can think about. It's all you can feel. It's all you know.

Now imagine being in a constant state of hunger, pain, thirst. When you can get past your physical state you are greeted by feelings of fear, anger, grief and hopelessness.

Imagine giving up your dignity, your identity, your will, your soul to relieve your seemingly endless suffering. What effects must such compromises have on a human being? It is no wonder the transatlantic slave trade, slavery, and the times that followed are usually given such short shrift in the recounting of our history. This is hard stuff. Far too many people say, "Of course the middle passage was bad. Of course slavery was bad. Of course Jim Crow and lynching were bad. Now let's move on." Rarely are people willing to look at what 'bad' really was.

In the pages that follow I hope to make real some of the experiences of our ancestors. It is important in this chapter that you try to feel what they might have gone through. We need to do this in order to learn and appreciate our history. We need to do this in order to get a stronger sense about the forces that have shaped our community. Finally, we need to do this so we can understand the strength our people had in order to survive and at times even thrive in some of the harshest conditions . . . strength that has been passed down to us.

The Maafa

The Trans-Atlantic slave trade, referred to as the "middle passage," marks a period of human trauma rarely equaled. The middle passage describes one leg of the triangular route of trade that brought captured African men, women and children to the Americas and enslaved them. Millions were forced onto cargo ships bound for unknown lands that included Brazil, the West Indies, Europe and the United States, among others. These people were loaded onto ships and crammed together with sometimes less than 18 inches between them. Here they would dwell for many weeks to several months in the bowels of the ship. They were deprived of any human comfort and shared in a collective misery. This disgusting place was where they slept, wept, ate, defecated, urinated, menstruated, vomited, gave birth and died.

It has been estimated that the millions of Africans that died *en route* exceeded the number of those killed in the Jewish holocaust of the 1930's and 40's. Yet few of us are even aware that this part of African American history exists. The first African slaves were captured and brought to Portugal in 1444. The first slaves were brought to North America in 1619, almost 400 years ago. Although slavery has long been a part of human history, American chattel slavery represents a case of human trauma incomparable in scope, duration and consequence to any other incidence of human enslavement. The fact that the delegation from the United States walked out of the United Nations World Conference Against Racism in August of 2001, a conference that declared American chattel slavery as a 'crime against humanity,' only served to highlight America's refusal to acknowledge this period in her own past.

This transatlantic exploitation is now being referred to as the "Black Holocaust" or the "Maafa," which in the Swahili language means disaster, calamity, or catastrophe. Up until recently, American historians have been unwilling to confront the realities of this 'great suffering' as evidenced by the usual absence of these events from our public school curricula and textbooks.

Though a full accounting of the story of slavery and the slave trade has yet to make its way into our schools and our social consciousness, in the last few decades they have become hot topics of research in the halls of academia. The subject of how many Africans were transported to the Americas along the Middle Passage has been a contentious issue for many scholars. In his 1969 study, *The Atlantic Slave Trade: A Census*, Phillip Curtin placed the number of blacks transported across the ocean at 8 million.[19] Most studies since then have increased this estimate. For example, Hugh Thomas's 1997 work, *The Slave Trade: The Story of the Atlantic Slave Trade, 1440-1870*, puts the number of Africans that arrived in the Americas at approximately 11 million.[20] More recent studies that have used documented evidence, such as ship manifests, as their basis, have placed their estimates at between 10 and 15 million.

Many Africans died during the Maafa. How many? Most scholars agree that nearly as many Africans died over the course of the Middle Passage as reached the end of the voyage. If this is true, then it is likely that between 10 and 15 million died on the voyage And this does not account for the millions of Africans estimated to have died fighting against their would-be captors who never made it to the slave ships. The actual number of those who died in Africa and en route to the Americas will never be known. However, the fact that millions perished is not difficult to conceive given the horrific and vile conditions aboard the slave ships. In some cases when there was an acute outbreak of disease like small pox or dysentery, ships were abandoned at sea with their human cargo chained helplessly below, destined to suffer a slow merciless death. Slaves who fought against their captors were murdered; others took their own lives rather than be resigned to a life of brutality and torture. And the suffering certainly didn't end for those who survived the journey.

Life in Bondage

Let's be clear: Bondage is antithetical to humanity. Therefore, bondage in any form is abusive. When we discuss living enslaved we are discussing only degrees of abuse. I have actually heard people attempt to justify slavery by arguing that many slaves didn't have it so bad. They claim some were even treated extremely well and were better off than people who were destitute and left to their own devices. All I can say is these people are the worst of hypocrites, for who among them would willingly give up their freedom under any condition?

Once again, let me be perfectly clear about this: Slavery by its very nature is abusive and abhorrent to the human spirit. It was no accident that the State of New Hampshire adopted the motto "Live Free or Die." Freedom means that much to us all.

It is detestable that constitutions were written and laws were enacted to develop and maintain the institution of slavery. Slaves had not even the simplest of human rights. They were chattel, defined as "a moveable item of personal property," and as chattel, slave owners were free to do with them as they pleased. As noted above, slave masters' rights to abuse those in their charge were codified with laws such as Virginia's "Casual Killing Act" of 1705 and its "Unlawful Assembly Act" of 1680, which among other things made it legal to kill a slave "who raises a hand against any Christian."

Being whipped until skin peeled off. Being worked to exhaustion day after day. Being beaten. Being deprived of food and water. Being raped repeatedly. Being considered less than livestock and treated worse. Welcome to the life of a slave. "But most slaves weren't whipped, raped or tortured daily. Most days were relatively uneventful," I've heard people argue. Yes, I'm sure that was often the case. So tell me how many times does a person have to be brutalized to be traumatized? What is the number of rapes an average woman must endure before we can assume that she is impacted?

And so far we have only considered physical assaults. Every day of a slave's life was an assault on their dignity, their humanity, their soul. The simple act of calling another man master is degrading and demeaning. How much more so saying it to someone for whom you have only hatred and loathing.

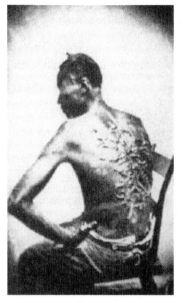

Results of Overseer beating

Rape

Rather than cursorily addressing the many forms of brutality slaves experienced, I decided I would write more in depth about two aspects of the barbaric treatment visited upon African slaves: rape and experimentation.

I searched for a way to approach writing this section that flowed and made sense. I struggled to find an opening statement, an anecdote, or quotation. I decided to start off by sharing the frequency in which white slave masters exercised their 'sexual privileges' on slave girls, girls that rarely reached their early teens without having been sexually abused, and to talk about the laws that stated,

> *"no white could ever rape a slave woman"* . . .*"The regulations of law, as to the white race, on the subject of sexual intercourse do not and cannot, for obvious reasons, apply to slaves; their intercourse is promiscuous". . So black women were perceived to be animal-like. The early English had believed that Black women copulated with chimpanzees or what were thought to be orangutans.* [21]

It was already, within the law to beat, torture, sell and accidentally kill slaves, so rape, of course, was a natural fit! Dorothy Roberts, in her book, *Killing the Black Body*, writes,

> *The fact that white men could profit from raping their female slaves does not mean that their motive was economic. The rape of slave women by their masters was primarily a weapon of terror that reinforced whites' domination over their human property. Rape was an act of physical violence designed to stifle black women's will to resist and to remind them of their servile status.* [22]

What must it have been like? Imagine that there is a slave mother with young children, among them a daughter about 10 or 12 years old. Like any good mother, she would want to protect her children from harm. Because she is a slave, her children are also slaves and she must come to grips with the fact that she is incapable of defending them against assaults from masters and overseers. This slave mother knows there will be a day when white men will demand to have access to her daughter and that these men or boys will use her fragile young body to satisfy their sexual cravings. That day may mark the initiation into manhood for the slave master's son, or perhaps that day she will be offered as an evening gift for white male visitors. The mother no doubt anguishes over this fact but still she hopes to lessen the tragic event by at least acquainting her innocent child with the particulars of being raped. She tries to help her little girl understand what will happen and why it is happening at all. She endeavors to explain how it will feel, how her vagina will tear, burn and bleed. She attempts to tell her how best to prepare and survive the ordeal; tells her to lie still, to not resist and to try to bear the pain. But there are limits to what she can tell her child to better prepare her. She cannot tell her how often they will come, how long it will last, or how many there will be. This mother cannot protect her. Nor can the father, who looks on powerless, defeated and emasculated.

The business of raping slaves may conjure up pictures of cruel and lascivious rednecks, cross-burning racists, fully draped in Klansman garb. The truth is those who participated in these rapacious acts were most often men and women of stature and prominence like the famous doctor James Marion Sims, the founder of modern gynecology.

Barbarism in the Name of Science

J. Marion Sims was a physician in the mid- 1800's who was credited with the creation of the first vaginal speculum. Sims built a makeshift hospital in his backyard where he conducted surgical experiments on countless un-anesthetized African slave women. Sims reasoned that slave women were able to bear great pain because their 'race' made them more durable, and thus they were well suited for painful medical experimentation.

Terri Kapsalis in her book, *Public Privates: Performing Gynecology from Both Ends of the Speculum*, discussed the prevailing view of black women among many southern physicians.

Their first pathological symptom was their primary racial characteristic: their skin color. In a medical world that categorized life as either normal or pathological, people of the African Diaspora were continually condemned to the category of pathological, their 'abnormal' skin color serving as a foil for 'normal' white skin. Pathological causes for this condition were concocted in order to explain its prevalence. Sander Gilman explains, "Medical tradition has a long history of perceiving this skin color as the result of some pathology. The favorite theory, which reappears with some frequency in the early nineteenth century, is that the skin color and attendant physiognomy of the black are the

result of congenital leprosy." Such medical arguments, in collusion with racist and stereotypic scientific and cultural explanations and excuses, provided the grounds for differential 'treatment.'[23]

The second symptom of pathology according to Kapsalis was gender. Black females were perceived to be irreligious, lustful, and immoderate. Their protruding buttocks and genitals were offered as physical evidence of their pathology. This was in stark contrast to white females who, while still thought of as pathological, were perceived as fragile and frigid.

So, where did Sims get all those slave women on whom to run his experiments? Many of the women came from slave owners who complained to Sims that these slave women were 'not fit for duty.' They were said to suffer from a particular disorder called a 'fistula.' An obstetric fistula is the breakdown of tissue in the vaginal wall, frequently as the result of childbirth, which affects the bladder and/or the rectum. The disorder causes leakage of urine and feces into the vagina, which made for a smelly and humiliating existence for the women. However, this condition did not preclude these slave women from participating in their daily work on the plantation, such as picking cotton, house cleaning, cooking, etc. So what duty were the women then unfit for?

The obvious answer is that while black slave women were required to do manual labor alongside of their black male counterparts, one of their other inescapable duties was to sexually serve their slave masters. Their malodorous condition made them less sexually desirable and thus, they were 'unfit for duty.'

Slave women were not the only group to suffer under Sims' reign; black infants represent the most innocent of Sims' victims. Black infants suffered from what he termed "trimus nascentium," now commonly referred to as neonatal tetanus. Tetanus originates in horse manure, the likely cause of the disease in slave infants given their living conditions and their proximity to animal stables. Sims attributed the condition to the indecency and intellectual flaws of black slaves, together with skull malformations at birth. Sims attempted to treat this malady by trying to pry the bones in the skulls of the tiny infants into alignment with the use of a shoemakers awl (see photo).

It is not surprising most of these children died in Sims' laboratory. Though their deaths were unfortunate, all was not lost, for Sims then had free access to their bodies for autopsies and further experimentation.

Slavery provided wealthy white citizens the ability to 'purchase' a virtually endless supply of men, women and children to abuse in whatever manner their fancies bid them, for however long the slaves could survive; and all with total impunity.

The Illusion of Freedom

1863. We were free! The years of torture, brutality, rape and abuse were over! Joy! Relief! Elation! Oh, of course there was confusion and trepidation, sometimes even fear about how we were going to survive, but on the whole our ancestors were excited for their future. They were finally going to be able to reap the benefits of their own ingenuity, prosper from their own labor and share the fruits of American society. Hope reigned.

For a moment. Shortly after slavery ended, states rushed to enact laws to continue the subjugation of African Americans. At the same time, vigilante groups formed to ensure that blacks learned their place in the 'new' South. Yes, slavery was over and highly-regarded men like Sims and his peers no longer had free and unlimited access to African American women and children, but the beatings, murders and psychological abuse continued.

Institutionalizing Oppression

Black Codes and Exclusionary Acts

After the Civil War, despite the heroic efforts of black and white abolitionists, whose names and sacrifices remain neither celebrated nor acknowledged, embittered white Southerners were still concerned about regaining control over blacks, while many Northerners were afraid blacks would overrun their communities. The major problem was what to do with millions of blacks whose freedom had just been granted. The South's solution to their problem was the introduction of Black Codes in 1865, laws to control the movement and activities of those recently freed. Though the codes were worded differently in each state, their consequences were generally the same – almost every part of a black person's life was regulated.

Southern plantation owners needed laborers, so many states decreed that blacks had to work for any wages the plantation owners deemed fair. If a black man or woman was found not working they could be arrested for vagrancy. These codes set out what work blacks were allowed to do, where they could do it and what hours they could work. These codes prevented blacks from owning land, voting, suing and sitting on juries. Often these codes defined where, when and with whom blacks could travel.

Fortunately, within a couple of years, the Federal courts ruled these codes too harsh and overturned them, claiming that whites and blacks should be subject to the same laws and penalties. Even though the Black Codes only lasted a short period of time, it is easy to see how they set the stage for what was to follow. Whites were not going to sit idly by and let the Blacks prosper.

The solution in some northern states was the introduction of exclusionary laws that restricted the number of blacks allowed to stay in their territory. Oregon was among the states that enacted laws of exclusion and these articles from its constitution, adopted in 1859, were typical:

Article I Section 35 – No free negro, or mulatto, not residing in this State at the time of the adoption of this Constitution, shall come, reside, or be within this State, or hold any real estate, or make any contracts, or maintain any suit therein; and the Legislative Assembly shall provide by penal laws, for the removal, by public officers, of all such negroes, and mulattoes, and for their effectual exclusion from the State, and for the punishment of persons who shall bring them into the state, or employ, or harbor them. [24]

Article 11 Section 6 – No Negro, Chinaman, or Mulatto shall have the right of suffrage. [25]

One justification for the exclusionary laws was a fear by whites that blacks would intermarry with Indians and form an undefeatable army that would annihilate them. This was a commonly held belief during this period and was expressed frequently by politicians. Samuel Thurston was a delegate to the United States Congress from the Oregon Territory. Speaking before Congress in 1850 in defense of his Territory's Exclusionary Acts he argued the following:

. . .The negroes associate with the Indians and intermarry, and, if their free ingress is encouraged or allowed, there would a relationship spring up between them and the different tribes, and a mixed race would ensue inimical to the whites; and the Indians being led on by the Negro who is better acquainted with the customs, language, and manners of the whites, than the Indian, these savages would become much more formidable than they otherwise would, and long and bloody wars would be the fruits of the commingling of the races. It is the principle of self preservation that justifies the action of the Oregon legislature. [26]

The Peonage of Sharecropping (1866 – 1955)

After the war, the federal government was called upon by Northerners to confiscate the lands of plantation owners who fought against the North and redistribute it among the ex-slaves. The government refused, leaving almost all of the freed blacks desperately poor. In order to feed themselves and their families, many of them agreed to return to work the land of their former masters in return for a share of the crops they raised. The remaining shares would be used to pay rent and buy supplies. Unfortunately, what frequently resulted was 'peonage'– the unlawful pushing of blacks back into slavery through debt servitude.

These families, having no money, would buy the seed, tools, mules and supplies they needed from local merchants on credit. Some merchants would then charge exorbitantly high interest rates, rates that made it impossible for the families to pay off their debts. Other merchants would take advantage of the local sharecroppers' illiteracy and simply create false billing statements. Either way, at the end of the season when the accounts were settled, the black family would inevitably find that they still owed money and would then be forced to remain on the farm to work in order to clear the debt. The following year they needed to borrow money again for seed, livestock and supplies, and so every year their debt would increase; thus in essence, the family was re-enslaved. Sometimes this went on for generations. Blacks who attempted to reject or escape such unfair treatment would be jailed or fined. [27] Which brings us to . . .

The Convict Lease System

While most believe that the thirteenth Amendment abolished slavery and involuntary servitude, a loophole was opened that resulted in the widespread continuation of slavery in the southern states of America – slavery as punishment for a crime. [28]

With the overturning of the Black Codes, southern plantation owners once more found that they were without a cheap source of labor. At the same time southern states had their own dilemma: what to do with free blacks that had committed crimes. Building and maintaining prisons was expensive, and states' coffers were all but empty. The solution, rather than imprison those convicted of crimes, was to lease them to plantation owners, as well as proprietors of other businesses, for the duration of their sentence. In this way everyone wins: businessmen got cheap labor and states got paid.

Did I say everyone won? Well, almost everyone won. In the state of South Carolina, the work was so perilous for those under lease, and the living environment so intolerable, half of the individuals that were leased died within the first twelve months. Some authorities have estimated that as many as a quarter of all black leased convicts throughout the South died while still under lease. [29]

Their labor, of course, was manual and backbreaking. Convicts were starved, beaten, brutalized, at times even sodomized. They were worked to death in some of the severest of conditions. They slaved in fields, on railroads, in mines. If one died, the operator of the business would simply call the state for a replacement. Life as a leased convict was no better than life as a slave, at times even worse. After all, not only were they less than human, they were now criminals.

Or were they? Often false criminal charges were trumped up as a means of legally securing large numbers of free or cheap human laborers. Looking at a white woman could get you arrested for sexual assault. Walking on the wrong side of the street might equate to disturbing the peace. Not only were many blacks falsely arrested, they were convicted at a much higher rate and received much harsher sentences than their white counterparts. It seems many in the South were not quite ready to give up on slavery.

Only this time the public's conscience was eased by the assertions of politicians, police, and others in authority, that blacks deserved to be held captive, because of their inherent tendencies towards criminality. Such

Convicts leased to harvest timber in Florida
(Photo courtesy of Florida State Photo Collection)

ludicrous ideas were the inspiration for the concept of "the white man's burden." The white man's burden referred to white peoples' obligation to control, direct and 'civilize' all those they believed to be from inferior races . . . for their own good, of course. In this way these 'uncivilized' people could become cultured citizens ready to play their part in their own development. Charles A. Ellwood in his 1913 book *Sociology and Modern Social Problems*, wrote in a chapter entitled "The Negro Problem,"

> *The problem of the Negro and of the Indian, and of all the uncivilized races, is essentially the same. The problem is, how a relatively large mass of people, inferior in culture and perhaps also inferior in nature, can be adjusted relatively to the civilization of a people much their superior in culture; how the industrially inefficient nature man can be made over into the industrially efficient civilized man.* [30]

'The Convict Lease System' began in Alabama in 1846 and spread throughout the ex-slave states soon after the war. It should be noted that while the system was not originally designed for blacks, it eventually became another tool for their re-enslavement after emancipation Convict leasing was so successful that by 1898 nearly three quarters of Alabama's total state revenue came directly from this institution. Other states that employed this practice reaped similar benefits until its eventual end in 1928. But it did not end. Convict lease rapidly was replaced by chain gangs; a similarly brutal form of forced labor which continued until its final abolishment in the 1950's. For almost 100 years after emancipation southern wealth continued to be built on the backs of what amounted to a slave workforce.

Jim Crow (1896-1954)

Dr. Martin Luther King Jr. knew first hand about segregation and its connection with a long tumultuous past, a past taught to him by his mother in his early boyhood and his mother's teachings stayed with him throughout his life.

> *Every parent at some time faces the problem of explaining the facts of life to his child. Just as inevitably, for the Negro parent, the moment comes when he must explain to his offspring the facts of segregation. My mother took me on her lap and began by telling me about slavery and how it had ended with the civil war. She tried to explain the divided system of the South - the segregated schools, restaurants, theaters, housing; the white and colored signs on drinking fountains, waiting rooms, lavatories - as a social condition rather than a natural order. Then she said the words that almost every Negro hears before he can yet understand the injustice that makes them necessary: 'You are as good as anyone.''* [31]

The ability to continue controlling and removing blacks away from white contact was now enacted via a new legislative policy that soon came to be known as Jim Crow laws – separate but 'equal' living conditions for African Americans, the American brand of Apartheid. The conditions for blacks were indeed separate; however they were rarely equal. What did surface were policies of outright discrimination that banned African Americans from public and private institutions, places of amusement, recreation and even places of worship. Included in this restriction were 'miscegenation' laws making interracial marriage a criminal offense, sending the strong message that the state believed blacks were so inferior to whites that mixing would threaten the survival of the white race. It is hard to see what their problem was; they had been sexually exploiting slave women and children for the past 240 plus years. According to an 1860 census there were close to 600,000 mixed race children resulting from white slave masters' sexual encounters with black female slaves. [32]

Ending Jim Crow: MLK meets with LBJ

But Jim Crow did not stop there. What the Fourteenth and Fifteenth Amendments gave, Jim Crow took away. The Fourteenth Amendment officially made African Americans citizens of the United States, making it illegal for any state to deprive any individual of life, liberty or property without due process of law. The Fifteenth Amendment ensured that all black males had the right to vote. Jim Crow changed all this.

> *Almost all southern states passed statutes restricting suffrage in the years from 1871 to 1889. Various registration laws, such as poll taxes, were established in Georgia in 1871 and 1877, in Virginia in 1877 and 1884, in Mississippi in 1876, in South Carolina in 1882, and in Florida in 1888. The effects were devastating. Over half the blacks who voted in Georgia and South Carolina in 1880 vanished from the polls in 1888. The drop in Florida was 27 percent. In places like Alabama, for example, where blacks equaled almost half the population, no African Americans were sent to the legislature after 1876. [33]*

And when black men did vote in southern states, many of their ballots were stolen, tallied in favor of opposing candidates, or simply not counted. (Not unlike what has happened in recent elections in some states today.) By the end of the century most southern states had systematically disfranchised black males by imposing even more voter restrictions, such as literacy tests and poll taxes. These new rules of the political game were used by white registrars to deny voting privileges to blacks at the registration place rather than the ballot box, a denial previously accomplished by fraud and force.

With the validation of the 'Separate but Equal' doctrine by the United States Supreme Court in the matter of Plessey vs. Ferguson in 1896, Jim Crow became the law throughout every state of the old Confederacy. Every aspect of life where blacks and whites might meet and interact was segregated, and with the systematic disenfranchisement complete, it was all but impossible for blacks to seek legal redress for any grievance.

Where governmental institutions left off, individuals and mobs continued. As blacks explored their new-found freedoms they began to set up schools, businesses and houses of worship. They began to vote, help pass civil rights laws and elect people to office. They began to prosper. This did not sit well with southern whites, so to insure that they maintained their illusion of supremacy, groups like the Ku Klux Klan (KKK) were established. Enrolling as members politicians, judges, law enforcement officials and business owners as well as poor whites trying to make it in the post-war south, these groups happily continued the traditions of their predecessors: rape, arson and murder in the name of state, skin color and God. If they could no longer legalize blacks into submission, they would terrorize them.

Once again, rather than present a litany of abuses I will focus on just a few, beginning with one of the worst: lynchings.

Strange Fruit: Black Lynching

Strange Fruit

Southern trees bear strange fruit, Blood on

the leaves and blood at the root, Black bodies

swinging in the southern breeze, Strange

fruit hanging from the poplar trees. Pastoral

scene of the gallant South,

The bulging eyes and the twisted mouth,

Scent of magnolias, sweet and fresh,

Then the sudden smell of burning flesh.

Here is fruit for the crows to pluck,

For the rain to gather, for the wind to suck,

For the sun to rot, for the trees to drop,

Here is a strange and bitter crop.

(Lewis Allen & Billie Holiday)

The right to vote and the freedom to vote are two very different things. Immediately after blacks got the right to vote, Southerners started fearing their domination. Soon the 'unwritten law' was in place that justified any acts of resistance. The KKK and groups like it vowed to suppress blacks' freedoms and proceeded to beat, exile and kill them. While lynching seemed to be the method of choice, individuals and mobs were not averse to drowning, shooting, stabbing, or burning. Any method would do. At first these terrorists' goal was disenfranchisement. Once that was achieved the terrorism continued.

Black men were killed for any number of reasons. They were killed for fighting with white men. They were killed for disputing terms of contracts with white employers. Sometimes they were killed for simply being what was often called 'uppity,' for simply standing up for themselves. Black women were murdered because they refused to tell the mobs where relatives could be found for 'lynching bees.' Black males, even boys just into their teens, were lynched for simply being accused of 'looking the wrong way' at white women. In fact, black men, women and children were lynched for all kinds of crimes—and for no crimes at all. Men and women were put to death at the whim of a mob. Neither judge nor jury was needed. Though we were now living as free men and women, with the same rights guaranteed all citizens of the land, we were being murdered at wholesale rates with the blessings of state and local governments.

A large number of those lynched were black men charged with improper encounters with white women. Although the most common charge was rape, black men were frequently lynched for insulting or just startling white women. Some were even lynched because a white woman claimed that a black man scared or intimidated her by looking menacingly at her. Ida B. Wells-Barnett in her 1900 article, "Lynch Law in America," describes the laws of the day.

> During the last ten years a new statute has been added to the "unwritten law." This statute proclaims that for certain crimes or alleged crimes no negro shall be allowed a trial; that no white woman shall be compelled to charge an assault under oath or to submit any such charge to the investigation of a court of law. The result is that many men have been put to death whose innocence was afterward established; and to-day, under this reign of the "unwritten law," no colored man, no matter what his reputation, is safe from lynching if a white woman, no matter what her standing or motive, cares to charge him with insult or assault. [34]

This was the repeated theme that found its way into the mass media with the airing of D. W. Griffith's film, *The Birth of a Nation*, which shows a white man in 'blackface' attacking a white woman who throws herself over a cliff in order to avoid being raped. The black character was calculatingly depicted as the evil villain. This contributed to the belief of many in this country that whites living in areas with substantial black populations lived in grave danger on a daily basis, as if they were surrounded by wild animals.

And whites in America and throughout the world accepted this view of blacks with little question. "The boy only got what he deserved" was a common refrain of onlookers after a lynching. How many times was such a proclamation uttered with sadness and pity, as if the 'good Christian' people responsible really wished things would have turned out otherwise. How many times did such pious souls deem it right and proper that a human being should be seized by a mob and burned to death upon the unsworn and the uncorroborated charge of his accuser?

Repeatedly, in a nation of laws that presumes every man innocent until he is proven guilty, white criminals blackened their faces and felt they could freely commit any crime so long as they were able to throw suspicion on a black person. After their escapades, these same criminals would then lead an angry mob in the pursuit of justice. Once again from her 1900 article, Ida B. Wells describes lynching in grim detail:

The world looks on and says it is well. Not only are two hundred men and women put to death annually, on the average, in this country by mobs, but these lives are taken with the greatest publicity. In many instances the leading citizens aid and abet by their presence when they do not participate, and the leading journals inflame the public mind to the lynching point with scare-head articles and offers of rewards.

Whenever a burning is advertised to take place, the railroads run excursions, photographs are taken, and the same jubilee is indulged in that characterized the public hangings of one hundred years ago. There is, however, this difference: in those old days the multitude that stood by was permitted only to guy or jeer. The nineteenth century lynching mob cuts off ears, toes, and fingers, strips off flesh, and distributes portions of the body as souvenirs among the crowd. If the leaders of the mob are so minded, coal-oil is poured over the body and the victim is then roasted to death.

This has been done in Texarkana and Paris, Tex., in Bardswell, Ky., and in Newman, Ga. In Paris the officers of the law delivered the prisoner to the mob. The mayor gave the school children a holiday and the railroads ran excursion trains so that the people might see a human being burned to death. In Texarkana, the year before, men and boys amused themselves by cutting off strips of flesh and thrusting knives into their helpless victim. At Newman, Ga., of the present year, the mob tried every conceivable torture to compel the victim to cry out and confess, before they set fire to the faggots that burned him. But their trouble was all in vain—he never uttered a cry, and they could not make him confess.[35]

While black men made up the majority of those lynched, as mentioned earlier, black women did not escape this form of execution. In 1918, a pregnant black woman named Mary Turner was hanged, covered with oil and gasoline and burned.

As she dangled from the rope, a man stepped forward with a pocketknife and ripped open her abdomen in a crude caesarean operation. Out tumbled the prematurely born child . . . Two feeble cries it gave-and received for answer the heel of a stalwart man, as life was ground out of its tiny form.[36]

The typical official account of such atrocities read *"Death at the hands of parties unknown."* It is difficult to imagine anything more deplorable than these senseless acts of violence that usually went unpunished. However the following *Weekly Republican* newspaper accounting from Springfield, Massachusetts, on April 28, 1899, reveals a level of barbarism by whites rarely, if ever, acknowledged in American history books.

Before the torch was applied to the pyre, the negro was deprived of his ears, fingers and genital parts of his body. He pleaded pitifully for his life while the mutilation was going on, but stood the ordeal of fire with surprising fortitude. Before the body was cool, it was cut to pieces, the bones were crushed into small bits, and even the tree upon which the wretch met his fate was torn up and disposed of as "souvenirs." The negro's heart was cut into several pieces, as was also his liver. Those unable to obtain the ghastly relics direct paid their more fortunate possessors extravagant sums for them. Small pieces of bones went for 25 cents, and a bit of the liver crisply cooked sold for 10 cents. As soon as the negro was seen to be dead there was a tremendous struggle among the crowd to secure the souvenirs . . . Knives were quickly produced and soon the body was dismembered. [37]

Between 1882 and 1967 200 bills were presented before congress to outlaw lynching. Additionally, seven presidents urged congress to end the practice. Each and every time these efforts were rejected by the congress and lynchings continued unabated and unpunished. It was not until 2005 that the U. S. Senate offered an apology for what it termed 'domestic terrorism' against mostly black people.

Greenwood

In 1921 African Americans had managed to build Greenwood, a booming industrious town within Tulsa, Oklahoma that came to be called the 'Negro Wall Street' by the local residents. Segregated towns like Greenwood formed because it was often unlawful for blacks to own businesses in white cities.

The tensions in Tulsa were part of a national pattern during the teens and 20's, when city after city exploded in the worst racial conflicts that the country would ever see. Fear of black independence and self-determination took a Freudian form: of rape hysteria. In one town after another, racial violence was sparked by rumors that a Negro had harmed a white woman. This happened in Washington; Omaha Neb.; Kansas City, Kan.; Knoxville , Tenn.; Longview, Tex.; and Rosewood.[38]

Why were tensions exploding?   In large part because, in the face of more than 300 years of bondage, segregation and oppression African Americans were organizing, building healthy and economically self-sustaining communities. Against overwhelming odds they were becoming successful.   For a multitude of reasons white society could not sit casually by and watch us flourish. So, in one of the most successful black communities seen in America up until that time it seemed like something had to give.

One morning during rush hour people claimed they heard Sarah Page, a white elevator operator scream and then saw Dick Roland, a black shoe-shiner, running from the elevator. As a result Roland was arrested and jailed for assaulting a white woman. The next day an article and editorial in the local newspaper called for Roland to be lynched. That night a white mob went to the courthouse to get Roland and a group of black men marched in from Greenwood to protect him. A confrontation between the groups ensued, shots were fired and the riot began. As the black men retreated to their community, white police officials deputized many of the mob and gave them instructions to, in effect, "go out and kill you some damn niggers." Perhaps as many as 10,000 whites stormed Greenwood. When it was all over, Greenwood had been razed to the ground and hundreds were dead. Ironically, Sarah Page refused to press charges against the accused and Dick Roland was acquitted. [39]

Once again, the familiar theme of a white woman being raped spurned a reign of terror by thousands of whites that left hundreds of people dead, the majority of whom were black, and the prosperous segregated black town of Greenwood burned to the ground.

Tuskegee

Seemingly, in the tradition of J. Marion Sims, the United States government decided it was okay to run medical experiments on African Americans. From 1932 through 1972, the U.S Public Health Service used 399 African American men who were suffering from syphilis as human laboratory animals in the medical experiment known as the Tuskegee Syphilis Study. The majority of the men were illiterate sharecroppers from Alabama who came to Tuskegee complaining of fatigue. Contrary to popular belief the government did not give these men syphilis; they already had contracted it when they came to the institute. After tests were run, they were told by doctors and nurses, people they were taught to trust, that they were being treated for a blood disorder. In fact, they were not being treated at all. They were mercilessly left to degenerate with syphilitic inflictions of paralysis, tumors, blindness and insanity, inevitably resulting in death for many.

It is detestable that doctors and institutions both black and white participated in this experiment. However, the fact that the United States government oversaw such an experiment is inexcusable and barbaric. Over 100 of the men died from syphilis during the study. A number of the unwitting participants passed the disease onto their spouses and a few times their pregnant spouses in turn passed it on to their unborn infants.

The study was halted in 1972 only when a former Public Health Service worker blew the whistle on the project. It's amazing to think that the study might still have gone on until the last participant died almost 30 years later had it not been for that one Public Health worker with a conscience. The study was purported to be a way of learning what effect syphilis had on the body. Unfortunately, this could only be determined post-mortem. In 1947, only fifteen years after the experiment began, penicillin was discovered to be an effective cure for the disease. It was still withheld from the men for the next twenty-five years.

Lynchings; razing homes and businesses; medical experimentation. Imagine if the atrocities described above happened to your husband, wife, child, parent, sister or brother. Perhaps your best friend. How would you handle it? It has been estimated that between 1866 and 1955 more than 10,000 African American men, women and children had been lynched; many thousands more had been murdered by other means; and untold numbers of women had been brutalized and raped. Add to this the tens of thousands, possibly hundreds of thousands who received beatings at the hands of whites, many of which were handed out by the police, and it's easy to see that the end of slavery did not mean the end of trauma for black people.

Again, we have only discussed the physical violence visited upon these people. What about the psychological violence? What must it be like living in a community where your life is in jeopardy on a daily basis? Where you have to shuffle to survive? Where your dignity and pride are assaulted at every turn? What must it have been like being treated as a third-rate citizen in a seemingly first-rate society, a society whose benefits you are consistently denied access to?

In Search of Civil Rights: The Crimes Continue

One hundred years after emancipation, Civil Rights became a reality . . . more or less. Today Jim Crow is a thing of the past . . . well, mostly. Lynching is rare. Many fewer black women and young children are being physically brutalized. The majority of us have the right and the freedom to vote. So, everything is fine, right? Racism is dead. The playing field has been leveled. I cannot count the number of times I have heard white people, as well as a few black people, argue, "Race is no longer an issue in this country. After all, slavery ended one hundred and fifty years ago and blacks have had their civil rights for fifty years. Stop making excuses. It's time to move on."

Oh, were it only so.

I was born in 1957 to Oscar and Nellie DeGruy, both of whom were born and raised in Louisiana. My parents left Louisiana because they did not want their children to experience the discrimination and hardship they had endured. They knew they would raise us to be proud and to stand up for ourselves, to insist upon being treated fairly and respectfully, and for all of these same reasons they knew our lives would be in danger if they remained in the South.

I was born at a time when change was moving like a raging fire, laying waste to antiquated beliefs and doctrines. The turbulent sixties bring up fresh recollections for me of war, protests, riots, assassinations and movement for civil rights.

My first memory of the Los Angeles Riots was when I was seven years old riding in the car with my family. We were coming home from a family gathering. Everyone was talking and laughing when suddenly the car slowed down and everything got quiet. I remember seeing fires all around us and overturned cars with people yelling and breaking windows and running out of stores with food, clothing and televisions. Then a man ran up and peered into the window of our car as if he were looking for someone. He looked carefully at each of us. He then turned and yelled out the words, "Black blood" to a crowd of black people standing behind him holding baseball bats and pipes. He then motioned to my father to move along.

It all seemed surreal. I couldn't recognize my neighborhood anymore. There was a flurry of emotions flowing through me, a mixture of fear and awe. There were sirens going off in every direction. My father turned the corner onto 55th street. Our house was in the middle of the block. All of our neighbors were outside standing on their porches and in their yards looking in the direction of the fires and the mayhem. There was a strange ambivalence about the riots that everyone seemed to be caught up in. I remember hearing older people say things like, "It's a damn shame that it had to come to this for white folks to learn they can't keep treatin' people like they're less than them."

Civil Rights and Gaining Equality

But wasn't the Civil Rights act of 1964 supposed to make things right? Didn't it establish no more discrimination based on race, color, creed or national origin? Unfortunately, the crime here is that civil rights legislation fell significantly short of its intent to level the playing field and guarantee equality and justice for all. Robert Westly says it best:

> *A crucial but seldom considered defect of all civil rights legislation is the fact that it needs to be administered and enforced. Many Blacks (and whites, too) appear to be under some delusion that once Congress passes civil rights legislation, Blacks are protected from discrimination and white racism. Nothing could be further from the truth, as the history of Black Reconstruction clearly shows. Every measure passed by Congress during Reconstruction for the social and political equality of Blacks—with the possible exception of the Thirteenth Amendment—was subverted or made null and void before the turn of the century.* [40]

Andrew Hacker, in his book, *Two Nations Black and White, Separate, Hostile, Unequal,* assesses the social condition of America, identifying the entrenched separatism that is more often the rule than the exception:

> *Black Americans are Americans, yet they still subsist as aliens in the only land they know. Blacks must endure a segregation that is far from freely chosen. So America may be seen as two separate nations. Of course, there are places where the races mingle. Yet in most significant*

respects, the separation is pervasive and penetrating. As a social and human division, it surpasses all others—even gender—in intensity and subordination. [41]

Hacker argues that whites who embrace America as a nation fail to feel in any way responsible for its condition. They deem themselves to be above oppressing or holding down their fellow black citizens. On the contrary, they believe that blacks have oftentimes been given unfair advantages. They are oblivious to any privilege their being born white has given them. Hacker identifies the deep-seated and often unconscious nature of racism that is embedded in the psyche of Americans, which reflects itself in beliefs of superiority and inferiority today.

America is inherently a "white" country: in character, in structure, in culture. Needless to say, black Americans create lives of their own. Yet as people, they face boundaries and constrictions set by the white majority. [42]

Leveling the Playing Field in Education?

Equal opportunity in education remains a pipe dream. Some urban high schools around the nation report dropout rates as high as 60%. Inner-city and rural schools are withering from over-crowding and/or lack of resources while suburban schools and schools in affluent districts flourish. Here in Portland suburban schools have better facilities, computers and laboratories. In Portland it has been decades since a new high school was built. In comparison, at least six new high schools have been built in surrounding school districts within the last four years. This is not uncommon around the country.

Affirmative Action was supposed to be one of those policies that evened things out. From its inception in the mid-1960's, Affirmative

Action has been under attack. In the mid-1970's, Allan Bakke, a white male, twice applied and twice failed to get into the University of California at Berkeley's medical school. Bakke filed suit against the University claiming that his grades and test scores were better than those of minority students admitted under the school's Affirmative Action policy. In essence, he argued that he was a victim of 'reverse discrimination.' In 1978, the Supreme Court in a complicated ruling upheld Bakke's suit, and struck down using racial quotas in university and college admissions. At the same, time the Court ruled that race might still be taken into consideration with regard to admissions.

Bakke was just the beginning. In 1996, the voters in California approved Proposition 209, banning Affirmative Action altogether. Proposition 209 prohibited the state, local governments, public universities, colleges, schools, and other government institutions from discriminating against, or giving preferential treatment to, any individual or group in public employment, public education, or public contracting on the basis of race, sex, color, ethnicity, or national origin. As a result, African American enrollment at California state universities declined by 50%.

While Affirmative Action comes increasingly under attack, children of advantaged white families continue to get preferential treatment. Have you ever heard of preferences given to the children of alumni, donors and employees at elite private and public universities? [43] These preferences often result in under-qualified students, from predominantly wealthy white families, being admitted to the school. In some of these schools, many times the number of students are admitted each year through such preferences as are admitted through Affirmative Action. It is repugnant when politicians, judges and captains of industry, who have received this preferential treatment for themselves as well as their children, speak out against policies designed to give those of less privilege opportunities for advancement.

Equality in the Workplace?

Shakespeare once wrote, "What's in a name? A rose by any other name would still smell as sweet." What's in a name? Plenty, if you're trying to get a job in America. In 2002, Marianne Bertrand and Sendlhil Mullainathan, researchers at the University of Chicago and the Massachusetts Institute of Technology, wanted to measure racial discrimination in the labor market. Their study, *"Are Emily and Brendan More Employable than Lakisha and Jamal? A Field Experiment On Labor Market Discrimination,"* had quite interesting results. Their approach was simple. First, they sent out resumes in response to help wanted ads in Chicago and Boston newspapers. Half of the resumes they sent out had African American sounding first names such as Tremayne or Aisha, and half had white sounding names such as Emily or Brad. All other information was identical. Second, they sent out resumes differing in names as above, and also differing in quality of work experience; half had low quality and half had high quality work experience.

Over the course of their research they sent out approximately 5000 resumes in response to ads for a variety of positions ranging from clerical workers to sales managers. The results surprised some in this country and confirmed what many others already new. White names received 50% more callbacks than black names. Further, white names with high quality work experience received 30% more callbacks than white names with low quality experience. However, black names with high quality experience received no more callbacks than black names with low quality work experience. It did not even matter in ads where the employer advertised, "An equal opportunity employer"; they discriminated just the same. [44]

So I ask you, is the playing field level? Of course not. Unemployment among African Americans is twice as high as Americans of European descent.[45] Blacks earn approximately 75% that of their white counterparts. Whether you finished graduate school or have yet to complete high school, this remains fairly consistent, regardless of the level of one's education.[46] While African Americans are over-represented in occupations such as Hotel

Maids and Housemen, Postal Clerks, Janitors and Cleaners, Correctional Officers, Social Workers and Security Guards, we are most severely under-represented in occupations such as Engineers, Lawyers, Realtors, Editors and Reporters, Biologists, Designers, Photographers and Architects.

Representation Imbalance

Though blacks have remained under-represented in schools of higher learning, in the workplace and in the halls of power since our country's intention towards equality was declared in the mid-sixties, there have been a few venues in which we have had more than our fair share of representatives . . . the front lines in Viet Nam and in our prisons.

The Viet Nam War

Growing up, there were countless discussions in my house about the war, how black people were dying over there and still being treated like second-class citizens back home. As a child I remember overhearing the adults and my older siblings saying how, "Black people were good enough to send to war and be killed, but we couldn't get a job or be treated decently here." These words were etched into my mind though I didn't fully understand their meaning until much later.

I had relatives and friends who went to Vietnam and brought back stories of how the blacks and other people of color seemed to always be on the front line. Was this true? Apparently it was. According to David Coffey, in the *Encyclopedia of the Vietnam War: A Political, Social, and Military History*,

> *African Americans often did supply a disproportionate number of combat troops, a high percentage of whom had voluntarily enlisted. Although they made up less than 10 percent of American men in arms*

and about 13 percent of the U.S. population between 1961 and 1966, they accounted for almost 20 percent of all combat related deaths in Vietnam during that period. In 1965 alone African Americans represented almost one-fourth of the army's killed in action. In 1968 African Americans, who made up roughly 12 percent of army and marine total strengths, frequently contributed half the men in front-line combat units, especially in rifle squads and fire teams. [47]

Prison

Since 1980 the number of incarcerated men and women in the United States has increased between 400% and 500%. In 2004 alone the Federal prison population grew 7.2%. As of June, 2003 the Federal Bureau of Justice reported there were 2,078,570 prisoners being held in federal or state prisons and local jails. Half were African American. While African Americans make up 12% of the general population, we continue to account for half of the prison population.

According to the Bureau, stark differences in incarceration rates prevail: 1 in 21 black men were in prison as were 1 in 56 men of Hispanic origin, while only 1 in 147 white men were behind bars.

If incarceration rates continue their trends, 1 in 4 young black males born today will serve time in prison during his lifetime, meaning he will be convicted and sentenced to more than one year of incarceration ... The per capita incarceration rate among blacks is 7 times that of whites ... African American males serve longer sentences, have higher arrests and conviction rates, face higher bail amounts, and are more often the victims of police use of deadly force than white citizens ... Nationally, for every one black man who graduates from college, 100 are arrested. [48]

The powers that be would have us believe that blacks are seven times more likely to commit crimes than whites. Obviously, we still have a long way to go to be treated equally in the eyes of the law.

Coupled with such severe over-representation of African American males in the prison system has been the growth of the system itself. Since 1980 prisons have once again become big business. More and more prisons are being built with private dollars, and with the privatizing of construction and management has come increased use of prison labor in the market place.

Today, prisoners are making jeans, sweatshirts, toys and circuit boards. They make car parts, pack golf balls and do telemarketing. They even take airline reservations, and all for major corporations as well as the federal government. For their labor inmates typically receive as little as 30 to 95 cents an hour. Not only do these companies get labor for well below minimum wage, they get it without having to pay for unemployment insurance, healthcare, vacations or pensions. In 2000 80,000 inmates held such jobs. Twenty-one thousand of these prisoners worked for the federal government, up 14% from 1998.[49] And their numbers continue to rise.

Sound familiar? It's a kind of convict leasing, though somewhat kinder and gentler from systems past. While some argue that this may not be all bad, since prisoners are being productive and getting paid, still one has to wonder when half the prison workforce is black.

Trauma From Civil Rights to the Present

One evening in 1967 in Los Angeles, my two brothers were returning home from a friend's house when they were stopped by two white police officers about one block from our home. Both officers got out of the car and approached my brothers, who were 17 and 12 years old at the time. One policeman stepped up to my older brother, got nose to nose with him and asked, "What are you two niggers doing out?"

My brother attempted to explain that they were on their way home when the officer drew his pistol and pushed it into my brother's mouth and said, "Do you have something to say? Just breathe, nigger, and I'll blow your head off."

Just then the partner of the officer threatening my brother got a call from the dispatcher and as quickly as the police had appeared, they left. Terrified and humiliated, my brothers went home. It didn't take long for anger to replace the terror. The humiliation remains.

Violence against people simply because of the color of their skin still abounds. How many of us were beaten and brutalized during our fight for our rights in the 50's and 60's? In 1955, a Mississippi mob killed 14-year-old Emmett Till for allegedly saying, "Hey baby," to a white woman. Young Emmett was shot in the head and found in a river with one eye gouged out and his head smashed in. In 1963, the KKK bombed a church in Alabama, killing four children. The same year, white supremacists assassinated Medgar Evers. Five years later Martin Luther King suffered the same fate. Unfortunately, the success of the civil rights movement did not put an end to the hate or the violence.

In November of 1988, Ethiopian-born Mulugeta Seraw was on his way home in Portland, Oregon when three Skinheads jumped him and bludgeoned him to death with baseball bats. They swung away at him to exhortations of "Kill him! Kill him!" from their girlfriends. In June of 1998 three white men attacked and beat James Byrd, Jr. a black man in Jasper, Texas. After they beat him they tied him to the back of their pickup truck and dragged him around until his body came apart.

Just about every black man I know has been harassed by law enforcement officials. A number have been assaulted. Some have been murdered. Most of us are aware of the events that made national headlines: the beating of Rodney King in Los Angeles in 1992, the murder of Amadou Diallo by police in New York City in 1999, and the savage beating of Donovan Jackson, a developmentally disabled and partially deaf youth in Los Angeles in 2002.

Less well publicized nationally were the shootings of Kendra James in 2003 and James Jahar Perez in 2004 in Portland, Oregon. In both of these incidents the victims were black and unarmed. In both of these incidents the officers had many options. In both of these incidents the officers chose to use deadly force where it was not called for. In all such events the question remains: Who were these officers protecting and serving?

Incidents such as these happen in every city in America. Usually only those that are caught on camera in large urban areas make it into the national news cycle. Many of them make it into the local media. Whether or not they get run in print, discussed on radio or shown on television, almost all of them become hot topics of conversation within our families and communities.

When they do make it to television they are aired over and over again. How many times did we see Rodney King being abused by those officers? When my son was seven years old, after seeing one of the many replays of the Rodney King beating, he was so disturbed he asked me with trepidation in voice, "Mom, will this happen to me?" Again I ask, how many times does a person have to see and hear about others like him or herself being physically and psychologically brutalized to be impacted?

In my son's case it appears the answer was once. Ironically, when my son was 19, he and his friend were walking home when they suddenly found themselves surrounded by police officers with drawn shotguns, handcuffed, assaulted and later released having been found innocent of any wrong doing. His fear at seven was realized twelve years later.

Progress?

Brutality still exists. The unrelenting violence and harassment that we experience, both personally and vicariously through the media, serves to dampen much of the hope and anticipation that we will ever be full and equal participants in this land. While white people are less likely to call you 'nigger' to your face, are they any less likely to think it? African

American males are still accosted by police on a daily basis for no other reason than the color of their skin. How many African American males do you know that have been stopped and hassled for 'driving while black?' In 1999 an investigation in New Jersey revealed that black drivers on the New Jersey Turnpike were five times more likely than white drivers to be stopped by New Jersey State Police. [50]

Redlining still exists. There are still many areas of the country where black families are strongly discouraged from buying homes and renting apartments. Often realtors won't even let African Americans know that homes are available. Other times people who have places for rent will lie to callers who they believe are minorities.

Disenfranchisement still exists. In the 2000 presidential election, 57,700 Florida voters, the vast majority of them black, were denied the right to vote. For every election, Florida's Secretary of State puts out a list of all Florida's felons called a 'Purge or Scrub List.' Those on this list are removed from the voter rolls because they are felons, who do not get to vote in Florida. It has been reported that in the year 2000, 90.2% of those on the list were completely innocent of any crime. It was also reported that while the vast majority of those on the list were African American, only 2% of the names on the list were Hispanic.

This might seem particularly strange given that Hispanics make up 16.8% of the total Florida population and Blacks account for 14.6%. It actually isn't so strange when you realize that Hispanics are as likely to vote Republican as they are to vote Democrat, while Blacks typically overwhelmingly vote Democrat. During the 2004 election it seems like Florida was at it again. The 2004 Purge List contained tens of thousands of names. The vast majority again were black and this time only 62 were Hispanic, less than 1%; and like in 2000 most of those on the list were innocent of any crime. [51]

One-hundred and eighty years of the Middle Passage, 246 years of slavery, rape and abuse; one hundred years of illusory freedom. Black codes, convict leasing, Jim Crow, all codified by our national institutions. Lynching, medical experimentation, redlining, disenfranchisement, grossly unequal treatment in almost every aspect of our society, brutality at the hands of those charged with protecting and serving. Being undesirable strangers in the only land we know. During the three-hundred and eighty-five years since the first of our ancestors were brought here against their will, we have barely had time to catch our collective breath. That we are here at all can be seen as a testament to our will-power, spiritual strength and resilience. However, three hundred and eighty-five years of physical, psychological and spiritual torture have left their mark.

Chapter 4:

Post Traumatic Slave Syndrome

Who can imagine what could be the feelings of a father and mother, when looking upon their infant child whipped and tortured with impunity, and placed in a situation where they could afford it no protection. But we were all claimed and held as property; the father and the mother were slaves! . . . I was compelled to stand and see my wife shamefully scourged and abused by her master: and the manner in which this was done, was so violently and inhumanely committed upon the person of a female, that I despair in finding decent language to describe the bloody act of cruelty. My happiness or pleasure was then all blasted; for it was sometimes a pleasure to be with my family even in slavery. I loved them as my wife and child. Little Francis was a pretty child; she was quiet, playful, bright, and interesting. But I could never look upon the dear child without being filled with sorrow and fearful apprehensions of being separated by slave holders, because she was a slave, regarded as property. And unfortunately for me, I am the father of a slave. . . It calls fresh to my mind the separation of husband and wife; of stripping, tying up and flogging; of tearing children from their parents, and selling them on the auction block. It calls to mind female virtue, virtue trampled under foot. . .But oh! When I remember that my daughter, my only child, is still there, destined to share the fate of all these calamities, it is too much to bear. . . If ever there was any one act of my life while a slave, that I have to lament over, it is that of being a father and a husband of slaves.

Henry Bibb, 1849 (ex-slave)

What effect has our history had on our culture and our soul? While in Southern Africa in 1994, I was particularly drawn to the children in the villages who seemed to be both happy and active. It was usually the children who were seen herding the cattle in the early morning hours and caring for the infants in the late afternoons. They were purposeful in their daily activities before and after school.

I remember sitting in a small house in a village in Southern Africa called Ndebele. The living room was scarcely able to fit 20 people. However, standing in the corner of the room were about 10 or 12 children all huddled together, and ranging in age from toddlers to young teens. I remember how perfectly quiet they were for the several hours that we visited with the village women. They were so quiet I actually forgot they were still in the room. It was only when a small infant began to fuss and was quickly carried out by one of the teens that I remembered that they were still there.

The children seemed delighted to be able to share in the welcoming of us (African American women) to their village and home. There was not an instance that I can recall when they were instructed on how to behave or what to do. They were absolutely clear about their roles and responsibilities and were in no need of direction. Later, they joined us outside where they sang us songs and asked us questions. The children exhibited confidence, humility and security while their parents beamed with pride.

We later visited a rather unique village in South Africa called Onverwagt, which in Afrikaans means "unexpected." The villagers were the descendants of Africans that had been enslaved by the Dutch. After Apartheid had officially ended, these people remained as a blight upon white South African history. We were escorted by a middle-aged couple, Gilbert and Tabitha, who shared with us the legacy of the people of the village. They committed their lives to saving the people of Onverwagt, who were literally starving to death. They introduced us to villagers whose names were Elizabeth and Margaret and Mary, names taken from past slave owners.

This village differed drastically from Ndebele in that there were no tribal associations, because the people of Onverwagt were no longer connected to a tribe or a tribal language. Gilbert, who had learned all of the tribal languages of the surrounding villages in an effort to regain his lost connection with his South African roots, had an easy time of translation. The villagers of Onverwagt only spoke Afrikaans so he simply had to translate from Afrikaans to English. This was markedly different from our visits to native African villages where multiple tribal languages were spoken.

It was here that I experienced what felt to be a journey back to the American antebellum south. The women and men wore clothing similar to that of southern sharecroppers. They held their heads low and seemed unwilling to look any of us in the eyes. The villagers had social problems which bore a remarkable resemblance to those of urban America. They had problems with drug and alcohol abuse, domestic violence, crime and poverty. The sense of shame and hopelessness was readily evidenced in the posture and disposition of the villagers we met who commonly apologized for their lack of education. The children were unruly, dirty, and engaged in aggressive and sometimes violent play. This was in stark contrast to the poor, yet calm and gentle nature of the Ndebele children. Compared to the children of Ndebele, the children of Onverwagt seemed rough, agitated and desperate. They lacked the sense of self assurance and dignity that I had observed in the children from more traditional villages.

Like the people of Onverwagt, the conditions into which the ancestors of African Americans were 'unexpectedly' thrust were unfamiliar and inescapable. Slavery yielded stressors that were both disturbing and traumatic, exacting a wound upon the African American psyche which continues to fester.

Trauma's Effects

What are the impacts of generations of slavery and oppression on a people? In order to begin to understand the magnitude of this legacy on contemporary African Americans, it is important to examine the diagnostic characteristics of trauma. What are the effects of trauma on human beings? What does trauma look like? How does the trauma manifest itself?

If I shoot someone, say an attendee at one of my lectures, most would agree that the victim of the shooting would be severely traumatized. A gentleman seated a few rows away from the victim might be somewhat less traumatized. Someone walking in the hall that heard the shot could possibly be traumatized. Some family members of the victim informed about the shooting may be intensely traumatized, while others very little. There might even be a woman seated next to the victim who may not experience any symptoms of trauma whatsoever. This is because human beings react to events differently.

With the destruction of the World Trade Center in New York on September 11th 2001, many Americans, once again, became familiar with the term Post Traumatic Stress Disorder or PTSD. Lots of citizens were reported to be suffering from the disorder as a result of witnessing the destruction of those buildings and the deaths of those trapped inside. At the same time, while most individuals who repeatedly witnessed the news coverage of the towers toppling did not seem to suffer any enduring mental or emotional damage, some did. People do indeed respond to trauma differently.

With what is known about trauma, is it probable that significant numbers of African slaves experienced a sufficient amount of trauma to warrant a diagnosis of PTSD? Since there are no living African American slaves today I will have to hypothesize using current diagnostic criteria.

The Diagnostic Statistical Manual of Mental Disorders IV, Revised, describes features of disorders, reports the conditions which may give rise to them and lists each disorder's symptoms. These all help clinicians with making accurate diagnoses. However, it is not necessary for an individual to show evidence of all of the listed symptoms to warrant being diagnosed with a specific illness.

The following are a list of some of the conditions which give rise to mental and/or emotional traumas that justify the diagnosis of PTSD:

- *A serious threat or harm to one's life or physical integrity.*
- *A threat or harm to one's children, spouse or close relative.*
- *Sudden destruction of one's home or community.*
- *Seeing another person injured or killed as result of accident or physical violence.*
- *Learning about a serious threat to a relative or a close friend being kidnapped, tortured or killed.*
- *Stressor is experienced with intense fear, terror and helplessness*
- *Stressor and disorder is considered to be more serious and will last longer when the stressor is of human design.* [49]

It is important to note that the manual states that any one of the above stressors is enough to cause PTSD. So what about African slaves? Many slaves did not experience just one of the above stressors; rather, many experienced all of them! And the great preponderance of slaves were subjected to these traumatic experiences over and over again! Taking into consideration the fact that slaves brought to the Americas from Africa were exposed to a 'lifetime' of traumas, even with the fact that not everyone is traumatized by traumatic events, anyone with limited astuteness could surmise that a considerable number of African slaves are likely to have suffered from PTSD.

Today, those who are diagnosed with PTSD exhibit symptoms that may require clinical treatment inclusive of drug therapy. Some of the symptoms of PTSD include:

- *Intense psychological distress at exposure to internal or external cues that symbolize or resemble an aspect of the traumatic event.*
- *Physiological reactivity on exposure to internal or external cues.*
- *Marked diminished interest or participation in significant activities.*
- *Feeling of detachment or estrangement from others.*
- *Restricted range of affect.*
- *Sense of foreshortened future (in other words, does not expect to have a career, marriage, children or normal life span.)*
- *Difficulty falling or staying asleep.*
- *Irritability or outbursts of anger.*
- *Difficulty concentrating . . .* [50]

Remember, these are just some of the symptoms that an individual may exhibit having had direct or indirect exposure to a single traumatic event. What about those who experienced a lifetime of slavery? What symptoms do you think they must have exhibited? Today people can get treatment for PTSD. I don't remember reading about any counseling centers that were set up for freed slaves after the Civil War. The effects of the traumas were never addressed, nor did the traumas cease. African Americans have continued to experience traumas similar to those of our slave past.

Once again, even more impactful than the physical assault on their bodies was the daily assault on their psyches. Since the capture and transport of the first African slaves, those brought to these shores had to deal with systematic efforts to destroy the bonds of relationships that held them together, as well as continuing efforts to have them believe themselves to be less than human.

The maintenance of healthy and secure relationships is among the most important values within the African culture. So what do you think would happen if those relationships were destroyed and never allowed to fully take root again? If you were going to devise a uniquely cruel system of punishment, you could never have devised something more devastating and insidious than American chattel slavery because it absolutely, categorically destroyed existing relationships and undermined a people's ability to form healthy new ones.

Perhaps of greatest impact though, were the daily efforts of the slave owners and others in authority to break the slaves' will. Free will is at the core of being human. Can you imagine what it must be like to have your will assaulted on a daily basis? You live in a society that constantly reminds you that you are no different from livestock and in some cases less valuable. When you attempt to express yourself, you are beaten down. When you attempt to protect your loved ones, you are beaten down. You are beaten until you call the cruelest and most vile man you know "Master." And God forbid you attempt to be educated or think for yourself.

As a result of centuries of slavery and oppression, most white Americans in their thoughts as well as actions believe themselves superior to blacks. Of greater import, too many African Americans unconsciously share this belief. This is not surprising, for as I have outlined in Chapter Two, centuries of repetition and justification have gone into establishing such understanding. It is from the impacts of past assaults that we must heal, and it is from the threats of continuing assaults that we must learn to defend ourselves, our families and our communities.

Passing Down the Effects of Trauma

Upon hearing the term Post Traumatic Slave Syndrome some of my readers might think to themselves, "How could African Americans today possibly be affected by events that occurred so long ago? After all, African Americans are free now! In fact, they have been free for a long time!"

I have often heard European Americans irately say, "You know what, I didn't own slaves, okay? And I'm tired of feeling guilty about what happened over a hundred years ago, so get over it."

My response to them is that I am not a slave now, nor have I ever been a slave, and as far as I know, nobody I have known personally was a slave. The fact is, I don't have any experience of being a slave. However, 246 years of protracted slavery guaranteed the prosperity and privilege of the south's white progeny while correspondingly relegating its black progeny to a legacy of debt and suffering. It doesn't really matter today if either of us, black or white, directly experienced or participated in slavery. What does matter is that African Americans have experienced a *legacy* of trauma.

What is this legacy? How is it transmitted? The legacy of trauma is reflected in many of our behaviors and our beliefs; behaviors and beliefs that at one time were necessary to adopt in order to survive, yet today serve to undermine our ability to be successful. Remember the stories I told in the introduction? These are examples of behaviors that have been passed down through generations.

Beliefs can be somewhat harder to see, yet they are there nonetheless. I have a friend who has been working with teens for the past 14 years in both the African American community and in the affluent white suburbs. One day we were discussing the differences in his experiences and he told me,

"Joy, there is one major difference between the two groups that I have noticed. Both groups of teens I have worked with are very capable, both groups are made up of basically good kids, and both groups have aspirations for their futures. The biggest difference I have seen is that in their hearts and minds the kids from affluent families assume they will be successful; the black kids from less affluence do not make this assumption."

When I later reflected on his observations I knew that in far too many instances he was right. These and other such debilitating beliefs and assumptions are also part of the legacy of trauma.

The question remains, how are such effects of trauma transmitted through generations? The answer is quite straightforward. How do we learn to raise our children? Almost entirely through our own experience of being raised. Most of us raise our children based upon how we ourselves were raised. Of course there are things our parents did that we decide we'll do differently, but for the most part parenting is one of a myriad of skills that is passed down generation to generation. What do you think gets passed down through generations if what was experienced were lifetimes of abuse at the hands of slave masters and other authorities? What do you think the result would be if generation after generation of young men were not allowed the power and authority to parent their own children? What do you think the result would be if education was prohibited for generations? What do you think the result would be if the primary skills that mothers teach their children are those associated with adapting to a lifetime of torture?

Today we know that if a child has an abusive parent, the likelihood that he or she will grow to be abusive is greater than if that child came from a safe and supportive home. We know that if a child comes from a violent home, there is a greater likelihood the child will grow to be violent. We know that if a child comes from a home in which one or both parents went to college, there is a greater likelihood that child will go to college. We know that our children receive most of their attitudes, life skills and approaches to life from their parents. We also know that most of these are learned by the time they are five or six years old. What training did children in bondage receive? James P. Comer writes:

> *The slave family existed only to serve the master and in order to survive physically, psychologically and socially the slave family had to develop a system which made survival possible under degrading conditions. The slave society prepared the young to accept exploitation and abuse, to ignore the absence of dignity and respect for themselves as blacks. The social, emotional and psychological price of this adjustment is well known.* [51]

In most families the dominant male is the father. Who was the dominant male in a slave's life? The master was figuratively, if not literally, the father. It was the master who more often than not became the imprint for male parental behavior . . . and this imprint was passed down through the generations. At its foundation, this imprint was dominated by the necessity to control others through violence and aggression,

While some of what we learn we learn through direct instruction, the bulk of our learning takes place vicariously, by watching others. The individuals and families that survived the slave experience reared their children while simultaneously struggling with their own psychological injuries. They often exhibited the typical symptoms associated with Post Traumatic Stress Disorder. The children lived and learned the behaviors and attitudes of their often injured and struggling parents. Today, we are those children.

In addition to the family, the legacy of trauma is also passed down through the community. During slavery, the black community was a suppressed and marginalized group. Today, the African American community is made up of individuals and families who collectively share differential anxiety and adaptive survival behaviors passed down from prior generations of African Americans, many of whom likely suffered from PTSD. The community serves to reinforce both the positive and negative behaviors through the socialization process. For example, in the 1940's, families frequently suppressed any signs of aggression in their children, particularly their male children. It was an acceptable and expected practice in African American communities to severely beat unruly boys so they would never make the mistake of standing their ground with a white person in authority.

While the direct relationship between the slave experience of African Americans and the current major social problems facing them is difficult to empirically substantiate, we know from research conducted on other groups who experienced oppression and trauma that survivor syndrome is pervasive in the development of the second and third generations. The characteristics of the survivor syndrome include stress, self-doubt, problems with aggression, and a number of psychological and interpersonal relationship problems with family members and others. Yael Danieli, in the *International Handbook of Multigenerational Legacies of Trauma*, explains:

> *The intergenerational perspective reveals the impact of trauma, its contagion, and repeated patterns within the family. It may help explain certain behavior patterns, symptoms, roles, and values adopted by family members, family sources of vulnerability as well as resilience and strength, and job choices (following in the footsteps of a relative, a namesake) through the generations. Viewed from a family systems perspective, what happened in one generation will affect what happens in the older or younger generation, though the actual behavior may take a variety of forms. Within an intergenerational context, the trauma and its impact may be passed down as the family legacy even to children born after the trauma.* [52]

This, then, is how the legacy of trauma has been transmitted. Given our history, should we be surprised that issues of abuse, ineffectual parenting, violence and educational disillusionment, to name a few, continue to plague African American communities today? Many of these dysfunctional adaptations can be linked to the crimes visited upon our ancestors. These are some of the manifestations of Post Traumatic Slave Syndrome.

Post Traumatic Slave Syndrome Defined

Post Traumatic Slave Syndrome is a condition that exists when a population has experienced multigenerational trauma resulting from centuries of slavery and continues to experience oppression and institutionalized racism today. Added to this condition is a belief (real or imagined) that the benefits of the society in which they live are not accessible to them. This, then, is Post Traumatic Slave Syndrome:

Multigenerational trauma together with continued oppression and
Absence of opportunity to access the benefits available in the society leads to . . .
Post Traumatic Slave Syndrome. **M + A = P**

PTSS is a syndrome. A syndrome is a pattern of behaviors that is brought about by specific circumstances. The circumstances that produce PTSS – multigenerational trauma and continued oppression plus a real or imagined lack of access are outlined above. What is the resulting pattern of behavior? Well, there is not a single pattern of behavior, there are many. I have identified three categories: Vacant Esteem, Ever Present Anger, and Racist Socialization.

The Power of Belief

Before we examine the patterns of behavior associated with PTSS, we briefly need to discuss belief, because belief is intricately woven into the syndrome's fabric. Belief is a truly powerful thing, much more powerful than most people suspect. Our beliefs color everything with which we come in contact. They determine what we perceive and how we evaluate. They determine what we consider unlikely and what we consider possible. They shape our memories as well as our expectations. They strongly influence how we think and feel.

When the young begin believing that their future is bleak, they sometimes respond in ways that boggle the imagination. In the early nineties, the Washington Post reported that children who were living in some poor Washington D. C. neighborhoods were engaging in fatalistic behaviors. Children as young as ten years old had started to plan their own funerals, identifying the clothes that they wished to be buried in along with the accompanying music to be played. According to some psychologists, these children felt such hopelessness, it appeared they were no longer trying to triumph over death. They were instead reconciling themselves to it!

Many black people still believe that white people mean them harm. While this is true in many cases, it is obviously not true in all instances. A 2003 study conducted by the University of North Carolina at Chapel Hill found that African Americans were reluctant to participate in research studies. African Americans were fearful their doctors might use them as guinea pigs in research that might hurt them. They often cited the Tuskegee experiments as evidence of why they continued to be skeptical and suspicious.[53]

Beliefs can so color our minds that we become paralyzed, unable to move beyond our fears and doubts, thus limiting our choices. Blind to our potential, we wander aimlessly, searching for enlightenment, yet remain barred from the infinite possibilities that are all around us. The essence of belief's influence was captured in this passage from Proverbs,

". . .for as he thinketh in his heart, so is he."   *Proverbs 23:7*

Our beliefs are working for and against us each and every day. We believe what we believe and then perceive things in ways that 'prove' or validate our beliefs. The beliefs that evolved over hundreds of years of slavery and oppression are some of the most significant impacts of PTSS. The effects of some of these beliefs can be seen in the patterns of behavior associated with PTSS discussed below.

Vacant Esteem

Esteem has to do with worth and value. Self-esteem is the judgment we make concerning our own worth. Through the years there have been many ways people have tried to define and measure self-esteem. Often these definitions confuse self-esteem with self-confidence or self-efficacy. While self-confidence and self-efficacy have to do with our beliefs about how effective and competent we consider ourselves to be, self-esteem, though related, refers to our beliefs about our value, our value to our families, our friends, community and the world at large.

Very often people discuss self-esteem in terms of low or high. They imply that people who do not think well of themselves have low self-esteem and those that do have high self-esteem. In these cases, once again, they are usually talking about confidence and efficacy. It seems more useful to talk about esteem in terms of health. A person's judgment of their own worth can be placed on a scale of unhealthy to healthy. Healthy self-esteem is the result of an accurate and honest assessment of one's worth, worth being the degree to which one contributes. Contributions take many forms: spiritual, intellectual, emotional and material. All that matters is that a person's contribution improves life.

Measuring worth is a tricky business, yet we all can identify it when we see it. How much do you contribute to others' success? How much do you contribute to the work necessary to grow yourself so that you can make even greater contributions to your community? How much are you willing to sacrifice for the greater good? How willing are you to accept responsibility for your mistakes as well as your successes? How determined are you to persist when things get hard? How willing are you to let the best person for the job lead and happily support that leader? How often do you delight in others' success? To what degree is the world a better place for your existence? These are some of the questions we can ask ourselves to assess our own worth.

So, how do we develop healthy self-esteem? There is a direct relationship between the degree to which we as human beings participate in productive service to ourselves and others and the overall development of esteem. The groundwork for the development of esteem begins at birth.

I asked my husband to define what our newborn grandson's worth was. He paused momentarily to consider the question and asked me to explain what I meant by worth. I asked him "What is Nasir's value?"

He responded by saying, "He represents the potential and hope of the family. He represents the continuation of our family lineage and legacy. He represents the future generation."

What is clear is that my grandson has value to us despite the fact that he has not yet contributed in any noticeable way. It is with our belief in his value that the foundation for his esteem begins to be laid. In the first few months that foundation is built upon by simple smiles, hugs and kisses, later through words of praise and encouragement. By the time he is walking he will be given opportunities to serve and will be shown appreciation for his service. It may start out with asking him to pick up a toy and put it away. Then, as he grows older he will come to know his value both by his helpful acts and our family's expressions of appreciation. As an adult we expect him to do work that is purposeful and meaningful; work that contributes to our society.

In this way individuals arrive at their self-esteem: first, as a result of the appraisals of the significant others in their lives; later, as a result of having their contributions appropriately recognized; and finally, as the result of the meaningfulness of their own lives. Children and adolescents who are given little responsibility and/or great praise for meaningless actions can easily grow up to be narcissistic, having too great an assessment of their worth. Conversely, children and adolescents who receive little appreciation for the actual value of their contributions can easily grow up with an undervalued assessment of their worth, ultimately believing themselves to be of little or no value. In the best of worlds, children are given greater and greater opportunities to do meaningful work along with being given an appropriate level of appreciation for their contribution. In this way healthy self-esteem is developed.

Vacant esteem is the state of believing oneself to have little or no worth, exacerbated by the group and societal pronouncement of inferiority. Vacant esteem is the net result of three spheres of influence – society, our community and our family. Society influences us through its institutions, laws, policies and media. The communities in which we live influence us through establishing norms and encouraging conformity to society at large. Our families influence us through the ways in which we are raised and groomed to take our place, as our parents see it, in our community and society. When these influences all promote a disparaging and limiting identity to which we believe we are confined, vacant esteem can be the result. It is important to note that vacant esteem is a belief about one's worth, not a measure of one's actual worth. Vacant esteem, being a symptom of Post Traumatic Slave Syndrome, is transmitted from generation to generation through the family, community and society.

When the parents in a family believe themselves to have little or no value, it reflects itself in behaviors that can instill a similar belief in their children. This belief is passed down through generations in the form of unexamined, and often long-established, child rearing practices. Some of the extreme ways we have worked to make our children submissive and docile provide examples of established parenting practices that can contribute to vacant esteem.

At the community level, groups of people establish agreed-upon beliefs about their members' worth, beliefs that are reflected in the community's standards and values regarding acceptable behavior, educational attainment and professional possibilities. These standards and values translate into what achievements are believed to be practical and feasible for its members. Problems can arise when these standards and values promote counter-productive behaviors or inaccurately limit what is truly attainable.

For example, Booker T. Washington's vision for the appropriate role of African Americans in American society was that of tradesmen. Given the limitations imposed upon African Americans in the South, it is easy to understand how he came to this belief. Unfortunately, many in our community bought into the notion that this was all we should aspire to. In the mid- 20th century, the family, taking their cues from their community, also supported this notion, traditionally sending their girls off to become teachers and nurses while keeping their boys at home to learn crafts and trades involving manual labor.

Society contributes to the formation of vacant esteem in a number of ways, through its laws, institutions and policies, as well as through the media. African Americans have been and continue to be disproportionately represented in our penal institutions. African Americans often live in neighborhoods where schools are functionally segregated and lack adequate revenue to sustain them. In African American communities, banks charge higher interest rates on home and auto loans, as well as make it more difficult for African Americans to get small business loans.

The media contributes to vacant esteem's formation by frequently displaying African Americans as criminals, disadvantaged, academically deficient and sexually irresponsible. All these and more serve to influence how African Americans perceive themselves and so impact their assessment of their own worth.

So what are the signs of vacant esteem? What are some of the behaviors and attitudes associated with it? Consider this real life example: In the summer of 1992, two teenage boys – call them Carl and Dominic – got into an argument outside of a local high school in Portland. As onlookers watched, the argument, typically about nothing important, escalated until Carl, pulled out a gun and pointed it at Dominic's face. The muzzle was no more than a foot from Dominic's eyes. He remained perfectly still as he watched his adversary slowly pull the trigger. Click. The gun jammed. Dominic did not run. Dominic did not attack. Instead he said angrily:

"Do you think I'm afraid to die? I ain't afraid to die."

One of the witnesses ran to call the police as Carl worked at unjamming his gun. Someone screamed for Dominic to run as once again Carl pointed it at Dominic's head and pulled the trigger.

Click. Jammed again. Still Dominic didn't move. Again Carl worked to unjam his gun, for the third time he raised it up to Dominic's face and pulled the trigger.

Click. Jammed again. The fourth time the gun went off. Dominic was rushed to the hospital. The bullet went through his jaw. Miraculously he survived.

Most people looked upon this event as an attempted murder when, in fact, they had witnessed another suicide attempt by a young black man. Too many young black men are looking to die, and while there is little glory in putting a bullet in your own head, there is much glory in being killed in a shootout with rival gang members. These are desperate young men, believing that there is no hope of a future. They neither think nor care about their lives a year from now, let alone five, ten or fifteen. Few of them expect to live past their early twenties. Life for them is to be lived until they go to prison or get killed. The despair among many youth in inner-city communities runs deep. Many of them have seen more poverty, violence, and degradation than any child should ever see. They are not afraid to die. They are afraid to live. It is a testament to their strength that any one of them ever makes it out. Invited suicide is one indication of vacant esteem.

Another indication of vacant esteem is the effort to undermine the achievements of other African Americans. We all know this by its euphemistic name 'crabs in a barrel.' Whether we are talking about youth in school or adults in the professional world, there are those who seek to bring down those who look like them.

Associated with this effort is the difficulty that many African Americans have in celebrating the successes of other black people, particularly those we consider to be closer to our own socio-economic level. So many of us are typically very proud of people such as Colin Powell, Nelson Mandela and the Williams sisters, whose achievements are seen as exceptional and perhaps out of reach. Yet at the same time there are those of us that have difficulty feeling positive about the promotion of a peer or friend. This condition is exemplified by a saying found in the book, *Dyadic Communication*:

> *"If I am a molehill, then by God there shall be no mountains."* [54]

In general, the belief that one has little or no value produces behaviors that almost demands the devaluing of others.

Still on another note, I've often wondered why it is that African Americans feel as though one bad act committed by a black person reflects upon all black people. On numerous occasions I've been in the presence of black people when we hear a news anchor report a robbery or murder taking place. Invariably someone in the room asks, "Was it a black person?" And someone else says, "I sure hope it wasn't somebody black," as if to suggest that if the perpetrator was black, we all somehow share in a collective blame and a collective humiliation.

Or perhaps there is an assumption that the repercussions for this stranger's act would somehow negatively impact how we, who share the same skin color and/or ethnicity, will be perceived or treated by whites. Whatever the case, this tendency to take on responsibility for the behavior of the whole race is irrational and stigmatizing.

The little boy who couldn't stand to be looked at; the adolescent staring down the barrel of a gun; the lack of appreciation for the achievements of our peers; and feeling responsible for the entire community: all are just some of the indications of vacant esteem.

Ever Present Anger

I was in Louisiana visiting family and we had decided to invite some friends along to go to a movie at the local theater. There were several women and two young men. We sat in the middle of the theater taking up nearly an entire row of seats. We were unaware that we had separated two rows of white youth who were talking back and forth before the movie started. We were talking amongst ourselves when we began to see popcorn flying over our heads. The youths behind us were tossing popcorn at their friends seated in the row in front of us. After a minute or so of watching popcorn sail over my head I was hit in the side of my face by one of the pieces of popped corn.

The gentleman in our party seated next to me was in his early twenties, approximately 6'2" and 250 pounds, visiting from the south side of Chicago. He stopped in mid-sentence when he noticed the piece of popcorn hit me in the face. Those of us watching witnessed a distinct change in his body language and facial expression that indicated extreme perturbation bordering on rage. He turned and looked behind him at the whole row with menace in his eyes. The entire row became silent and motionless. As he began to stand up I touched his arm gently and said, "It was only popcorn." It was clear to me that had I not gestured to my young friend to remain in his seat he would likely have verbally and quite possibly physically assaulted someone.

But what could have prompted such a response from my friend? Was there a threat of injury? No. Was I in any immediate danger? Of course not. Yet the potential for violence was very present. Perhaps a more important question is, why did he become so angry so suddenly? What did he believe was really happening? How did he interpret the event? Why did he go straight to aggression as a solution? And what problem was he actually trying to solve?

We have all heard of events like this one. Some of us have been directly involved in them – where seemingly innocuous incidents become potentially dangerous for no apparent or rational reason. Even when we're producing quality work, laughing with our friends or enjoying time with our family, anger rarely is far away. It's as if there is a wellspring of anger that lies just below the surface of many African Americans, and it doesn't take much for it to emerge and be expressed. This seems to be especially true for many black men. This ever-present anger is one of the most pronounced behavior patterns associated with Post Traumatic Slave Syndrome.

So why is it that anger is such a large part of the experience of most African Americans? Are we an inherently violent people? How many times have we heard a variation of, "Slavery's over. You all have been free for nearly one hundred and fifty years. You are all blessed to live in a nation where all you have to do is pull yourself up by your own bootstraps, work hard and so become anything you want, even President. So why are you still angry?"

To understand why many African Americans become angry so quickly we first need to understand the causes of anger. Dr. James R. Samuels explains,

> *In its simplest form anger is the normal emotional response to a blocked goal. Often, if a person's goal remains blocked over time, they will begin to consider the possibility of failure and so experience fear, and when we are fearful we also lash out in anger.* [55]

So anger can be both a response to the frustration of blocked goals and the fear of failure. Lets see how this works.

A black executive who has been working hard for a promotion by putting in extra hours and excelling in his productivity and efficiency may feel angry when he is denied advancement by his employer. His goal of advancement was blocked and his response is anger. As a result, he is more determined than ever to get that promotion and becomes even more productive and efficient. Unfortunately, when the next round of promotions are handed out he is passed over again.

Now his anger is intensified because he likely is coming to believe his goal of promotion is no longer within his control. While some may consider simply working even harder for the next opportunity, when an individual experiences repeated stops despite great effort, working harder becomes less of an option and the resulting intensified anger can often escalate to hostility and sometimes even violence. When the executive believed he had a chance at promotion, his anger at being passed over was expressed as determination. Now his anger is expressed in the form of rebellion. The executive focuses his anger on his boss, rather than focusing on his goal of promotion. The deserving executive who repeatedly gets passed over for promotion could conceivably be angry enough to be overtly hostile; he almost certainly feels like it. If he thought it would do any good, he actually might express himself in such a manner, but he knows it would be counterproductive, so he stuffs his feelings.

Yet his feelings have to be addressed in some way. The executive may have some coping strategy that allows him to resolve his feelings. Given enough time his feelings may dissipate, only to reappear with greater intensity the next time a similar goal of his is blocked. Perhaps he has a wife that will let him vent and get it off his chest. But even the most understanding partner often times is not enough.

So what is the man to do? His anger and frustration have to find some outlet. Typically, when the true target of a person's feelings is deemed to be out of reach, the person will take their feelings out on safer targets. It is likely our executive will express his hostility where it is safest – on those closest to him, like his family or friends

Now, this executive's goal of getting a promotion is relatively insignificant when compared to the goals of insuring the safety and progress of your family amidst seemingly insurmountable obstacles imposed by those in power. What do you think might be the result when those goals are blocked repeatedly? Imagine the anger experienced by people simply trying to feed their families, live happily with a modicum of health, and be treated justly with respect and dignity in a society that on a daily basis frustrates them in pursuit of even these most modest of goals.

One of the most significant goals that have been blocked consistently by the dominant culture has been that of the African American community's integration into the greater society with all the responsibilities, rights and privileges concomitant with membership. William Grier and Price Cobbs, in their 1968 book *Black Rage*, point out that the history of slavery and the failure of America to successfully integrate its black citizenry into the social and political fabric of America, to allow them fair and equal access, has led to a very real and lasting rage in African Americans, especially in view of the lies perpetuated about equality of access by the powers that be.[56]

Blacks have been told lies about slavery; they have been told lies about being free, about inclusion, equality and justice; about the pursuit of happiness, security and prosperity; about civil rights, fair housing, education, and jobs. The lies have spanned centuries. What is most consistent is the absence of an accurate historical accounting of the illusive quest for equality and freedom for all of the citizens of the United States, especially those of color.

Now add to this a historical component and a more fleshed out picture emerges. Slavery was an inherently angry and violent process. White people modeled anger and violence in every aspect of enslavement. Individuals were forcibly captured, chained, and regularly beaten into submission over hundreds of years. Any group of people living under such harsh conditions would eventually learn the ways of their captors. Thus, Africans learned that anger and violence were key ingredients necessary to insuring that their needs were met. It was anger and violence that created and maintained the institution of slavery and this anger and violence continued long after slavery was abolished.

The slave family experienced a markedly different form of social organization than any other group on American soil. The individual and family were socialized to endure and survive under extremely oppressive conditions. Generations were born, lived and died enslaved in what has been purported to be the most free society in the history of the world with their struggle for freedom, respect and dignity attacked at every turn. These attacks continued long after slavery officially ended.

Today the African American family has continued to rear their offspring to survive in the face of a multitude of indignities, disrespects and blocked goals. Standing out among these are blocked opportunities for education through the systematic elimination of affirmative action policies and defacto school segregation, as well as blocked opportunities for economic self-sufficiency as the result of discriminatory bank lending policies, redlining and gentrification. Thus, much of the anger is a reaction to our hopes and dreams being continuously undermined by the institutions which govern us and the racism that permeates American society.

This is the experience of too many African Americans. It's no wonder we're angry. Even when we're feeling good, an ever-present anger resides just below our surface. Anger at the violence, degradation and humiliation visited upon ourselves, our ancestors and our children; anger at being relegated to the margins of the society in which we live; anger at the misrepresentation and trivialization of our history and culture; and finally, anger at living in the wealthiest nation in the world and not having equal opportunity and access to its riches.

However, our exploration of this subject is only a beginning. While gaining understanding as to why anger is seemingly ever present in the black experience is important, it is infinitely more important to explore ways we can transform this anger into something more productive and useful.

Racist Socialization

One summer around 1995 I was speaking to a group of high school sophomores about human sexuality and individual responsibility. Part of the course dealt with establishing healthy relationships and issues of gender. I was taken aback by one of the young men when he told me, "My mother told me to never bring home anybody as black as me."

The young man had the skin color of dark chocolate; it was smooth, blemish-free and quite beautiful, like that of his mother. My disturbed look must have shown clearly given what followed. Before I could respond, he said almost apologetically, "Oh, but I could bring home someone like you," meaning, of course, that I was fair-skinned enough to meet his mother's approval.

I explained to him how unfortunate it was that his mother had grown to believe that dark skin was something negative and that I did not feel complemented she would approve of my skin color.

I could only imagine how it must have felt for her, as a black woman, growing up and believing there was something wrong with her skin color, then having a child that served almost as a curse and a constant reminder of her own unworthiness. And what effect did this have on her son? Predictably enough, this same young man married a fair-skinned woman of another race, perhaps in hopes of escaping the stigma he had associated with being black.

It is not uncommon for people being held captive to take on the views and attitudes of their captors. At times, under the stressful conditions associated with being held captive, people can identify so closely with their tormentors they become like them. This transition has been known to occur after months of captivity and sometimes even after only a few weeks. So what do you think might happen to a people who have been held captive for generations?

One of the most insidious and pervasive symptoms of Post Traumatic Slave Syndrome is our adoption of the slave master's value system. At this value system's foundation is the belief that white, and all things associated with whiteness, are superior; and that black, and all things associated with blackness, are inferior. Through the centuries of slavery and the decades of institutionalized oppression that followed, many African Americans have, in essence, been socialized to be something akin to white racists. Many of us have adopted the attitudes and views of white, racist America. Many of us look at ourselves and our community through white eyes. We both mold ourselves to accommodate white prejudices and endeavor to adopt their standards.

This is made manifest in a myriad of ways. Many African Americans have adopted white standards, including those of beauty and material success as well as violence and brutality. Some of those who have reached the highest levels of American society have denied the role of the civil rights movement in their success; others consistently argue against the value of the concept of affirmative action. They have become akin to modern day 'overseers,' having fully adopted the white version of the American dream. They, like many of their white peers, seem to believe that slavery ended in 1865 and everything's been fine since.

At the same time some African Americans project an image of inferiority through their behavior, thus confirming the views of white racists who believe themselves superior. When so many of our youth glamorize thug life and lack of education, when their primary avenues of aspiration are athletics and entertainment, and when males and females, young and old, are sexually irresponsible, we make very real the prejudices of white America and give life to their caricatures of African Americans.

These and more are indications of racist socialization and it is easy to see how such socialization came about. From the time of their capture or birth, slaves saw whites as strong, rich, well-fed, secure and healthy. In relation to themselves, whites were perceived to be powerful and dominant. Slaves, of course, had the opposite qualities. Relative to whites, they were weak, poor, impoverished, insecure and unhealthy. Simply put, they were impotent and submissive. With which set of qualities would you wish to be associated?

Let's take an example: the pursuit of the white ideal of beauty. When slave owners had children by their black slave mistresses the owners would allow these offspring to work and sometimes live in their homes. Naturally, these slaves usually had lighter skin and straighter hair; and the lighter and straighter the better from the owner's point of view. Light skin and straight hair rapidly became associated with an improved quality of life.

During slavery thick wavy hair was referred to as "good hair" and kinky hair was relegated to being "bad hair." Ayana Byrd and Lori Tharps in their book *Hair Story: Untangling the roots of Black Hair in America*, write,

> *Good hair was thought of as long and lacking in kink, tight curls, and frizz. The straighter the better. Bad hair was the antithesis, namely African hair in it's purest form. White slave masters reinforced the "good-haired," light skin power structure . . . At slave auctions they would pay almost five times more for a house slave than for a field slave, showing they were more valuable.* [57]

Thus began the socialization of blacks to believe that dark skin and kinky hair were attributes to be loathed. In the mid-1800's, a black woman named Sarah McWilliams, better known as Madam C. J. Walker, became the first self-made female American millionaire after marketing hair growth products and a French made metal comb that straightened hair. Today this concept of 'good' and 'bad' hair still persists and both males as well as females continue to go to great lengths to cosmetically produce the idealized standard of white beauty, employing everything from hair straightening products to skin bleaching creams and in some cases even plastic surgery.

Another indication of racist socialization can be seen in African Americans' failure to celebrate the accomplishments of fellow African Americans. When viewed from a historical perspective, it is understandable why African Americans tend to feel threatened by the accomplishments of one another. As stated earlier, slaves were divided in many different respects: the house slave from the field slave, the mixed race slave from the black slave, etc. These different designations meant the access to, or the denial of, privileges and it was common practice for slave owners to set one class of slave against another.

According to slave narratives and other historical accounts we know slave owners perpetuated feelings of separateness and distrust by sometimes ordering some black slaves to beat or otherwise punish their friends, peers and relatives. Black overseers who were assigned the duties of monitoring and disciplining the field slaves were often more brutal than their white counterparts. One reason for their brutality was that thy did not want to be perceived as being lenient and so lose their position. Another reason was that slave masters rewarded them for their cruelty.

The racist socialization of African Americans began with slavery and continued throughout American history. Whites have consistently been portrayed and perceived as superior, powerful and right. For those who were educated and could read, book after book asserted that blacks, as well as other peoples of color, were dirty, lustful, stupid, immoral, incapable of reasoning . . . inferior to whites in every way. As movies became popular in the early 20th Century, blacks were consistently cast in the roles of servants and buffoons. Little changed with the advent of radio and later television. It was the rare exception when a black character was portrayed as a dignified, competent and caring human being.

African Americans have a unique socialization experience due to having centuries of systematic and traumatic programming of inferiority. This inferiority covered all aspects of one's being. In other words, from the beginning Africans were taught they were inferior physically, emotionally, intellectually and spiritually, thus rendering them completely ineffectual in their own eyes and the eyes of the society around them. At the end of slavery little changed in dispelling these notions. In fact, since the abolition of slavery such notions have continued to infiltrate all aspects of American life.

Vacant esteem. Ever present anger. Racist socialization. The effects of almost four centuries of legalized abuse, programmed enslavement and institutionalized oppression can be seen today. Centuries of slavery and oppression and the resulting Post Traumatic Slave Syndrome have impacted the lives of many, many African Americans. To believe otherwise is nonsensical. In the next chapter we will examine how PTSS has manifested in slavery's children.

Chapter 5:

Slavery's Children

For These are all our children.
We will all profit by, or pay for,
Whatever they become.
James Baldwin

During the Spring of 1990 I had the profound experience of being called to my father's bedside just before he passed away. This would be the last time I would see him alive. My father had always been a proud man, strong and clear about who he was. He called himself an 'Asiatic Black Man' long before black was considered beautiful in America. He once put a cousin out of our home because she was treating my brothers and sister and I differently based on our skin color. He actually packed her bags and put them on the front porch, then pushed them and her out of the door.

That spring day in 1990 my father trembled as he spoke, as if both nervous and agitated about what he was going to say. He began by saying that he wanted me to have his Masonic ring, which he took off of his hand and gave to me. He then said,

"There are some things I need you to know. The road of life is long and hard and you should not try to walk it alone. You need people to help you along the way."

The next thing my father said to me seemed strange and disconnected at the time, however, years later its relevance became clear. He began to tell me about his life, first as a young boy growing up in Louisiana. He recounted a story where he was walking along a dirt road down in the Bayou when some white men approached him and said, "Boy, you get over here and you load these boxes, y' hear me boy."

I noticed that my father was now becoming noticeably upset as he spoke. He was quiet for a while, then he turned to me and said, "And I did what they told me to do. . . . but I did it for you, Joy." Then he went quiet.

I waited through the uncomfortable pause wondering what could be causing what evidently weighed so heavily on his heart. My thoughts were interrupted as he began to speak again. He said, "When I was a young man in the Navy," he repeated and emphasized, "I was a man! Joy . . . when some white officers walked up to me and they said, 'Boy, get over here and peel these shrimp, and y' better do it now, boy."

I could clearly see the tears beginning to well up in my fathers eyes . . . a rare sight for a man whom I'd always known to be a pillar of strength. Once again he was quiet. And for a second time he repeated, "But I did it for you Joy."

I realized much later the burden that my father had carried nearly all his life, of being disrespected and humiliated both as a youth and as a man. I think my father's words somehow spoke of a deeper need to know that the daily assaults on his manhood, attacks that he had experienced his entire life, were not in vain. He sought solace in his belief that the birth of his children made it all worthwhile, for had he not tolerated the dishonorable treatment, if he had stood up in either instance, it may have cost him his life and me mine.

Still it was clear that my father suffered to his dying breath as a result of the indignities that had been heaped upon him, a disgrace that haunted him like an evil companion to the end. A burden he carried simply because he was a black man.

My father was not unusual . . . for a black man. As African Americans we all bear the burdens of our ancestry to some degree. And make no mistake: though some of us bear them more than others, all of us have been affected. Three hundred plus years of slavery and oppression certainly have had their impact. A portion of the impact has given rise to weaknesses that we have to understand, confront and deal with if we are to thrive. Another portion has provided us with great strengths upon which to build. In both regards we all are slavery's children.

So, what is the state of slavery's children today? How are the impacts of our past history visible? What are some of our behaviors that point to Post Traumatic Slave Syndrome? How are vacant esteem, ever present anger and racist socialization expressed in ourselves, our families and our communities in this new millennium?

Finding some of the answers to these questions lies at the very heart of PTSS research and study. Understanding how our lifestyles are influenced by those of our ancestors may open up new ways of addressing some of our most life-threatening problems.

Life and Death

Again, while African American's account for approximately 12% of the nation's population, we are dying at a disproportionate rate. African Americans have a life expectancy rate that is five to seven years less than that of whites. African American infant mortality rates are over twice that of whites. African Americans, per capita, lead the nation in the number of deaths caused by heart disease, diabetes, HIV/AIDS, hypertension, homicide, influenza and pneumonia.[61] We can easily add to this list issues of obesity, substance abuse and numerous cancers, all prevalent in our communities.

Additionally, African Americans suffer from all of the social ills that plague society at large: drug abuse, crime, and moral decay, to name a few. It would be foolish to argue that every maladaptive manifestation of these ills is a result of Post Traumatic Slave Syndrome. Still, it would serve us well to understand to what degree these and other problems of today directly relate to the slave experience of yesterday. Put another way, what adaptive behaviors have we taken on that have led to harmful habits, habits we are capable of replacing with healthier ones? Some of the things that have come to be associated with "black culture" are negative, demeaning and harmful, such as public displays of verbal or physical aggression at parties or various other gatherings, eating foods high in salt and fat, and adding sugar to nearly everything. These and many other behaviors have come to be expected and acceptable.

African Americans have unwittingly adopted habits and traditions that influence how we think, what we eat, what we believe about health and health care, how we manage interpersonal conflict and even how we behave sexually. No cursory view of African American lifestyle will explain the state of slavery's children. The exploration of our past's influence on our present forms the basis for PTSS work and research.

Who Are We?

At one time we have been considered chattel and at another slaves. We have been indentured servants and we have been sharecroppers. We have been called darkies, niggers, nigras, Negroes, colored, black, Afro-American, the intra-cultural colloquialism 'nigga' and most recently, African Americans. Each designation has a historical link that carries with it perceptions of ourselves and of our group.

Who or what we perceive ourselves to be is influenced first by those in our immediate environment that confirm and reinforce for us their perspectives.

Invariably our parents, families and friends play a vital role in helping us form our image of ourselves. Perhaps even more influential are all the sights and sounds we are exposed to on a daily basis in our communities. Our families and communities model for us how to be, who to trust and who to fear, how to work, when and where to play and who to play with. They teach us about power: who has it, (and that it is almost never them), and how to live, love and survive without it.

As influential as our families, friends and communities are to the formation of our self-concept, often the most influential contributor to what many of us come to understand ourselves to be is our society at large, as expressed by the media barrage we are exposed to on a daily basis.

Media's Contribution to Our Self-Image

The media has been a central vehicle for transmitting images to the masses. They control how the images will be displayed as well as who and what will be depicted. The media has been a powerful tool in shaping public perceptions of individuals and specific groups. They market what is acceptable and unacceptable to their consumers, guided by their stakeholders and more significantly, their stockholders.

The media images of African Americans are seared into the mental frying pan of its citizenry, swallowed whole and eventually go unconsciously down the social 'gut' of America. And what is ingested is rarely the truth. On the contrary, and more frequently, it is a carefully crafted hype designed to inflame and incite controversy, which sells newspapers and further divides America from Americans.

Take the Rodney King incident and the ensuing riots as an example. What percentage of those rioting were African American? Most people I have asked came up with numbers as high as 90%. This is understandable based on the news coverage because television and print media accounts largely presented it as an 'African American riot.' In reality, more than half of those rioting were Hispanic and the remaining were a mix of Whites, Asians and African Americans. It is difficult, if not impossible, to get an accurate assessment of one's 'group' if we must rely only on the information commonly available to us. Our schools, literature and mass media give an incomplete and often times intentionally misleading view of who we are as a people.

Having been a victim of false statements by the media, I am ever cognizant of the role media plays and has played in stirring up fear, hatred and bigotry, manipulating the public in order to increase ratings. Perhaps it is true that violence, controversy and tragedy sells, but at what cost? The media provides the lens through which we view others, whether people of color, criminals, the poor, police, politicians, or terrorists.

More importantly, the media is the lens through which people view themselves. Through the media, individuals with vacant esteem not only recognize their own impotence but are also shown their group and community's lack of power and efficacy. And all of this can occur in a thirty-second sound bite.

What happens to us, and to our children, when we are told by our parents that we can be, do, and have anything we want, that we are smart, strong and able, while at the same time we are accosted daily with sounds, images and experiences that tell us otherwise? Referring to a similar contradiction, in *The Souls of Black Folk*, W.E.B. DuBois wrote,

It is a peculiar sensation, this double-consciousness, this sense of always looking at one's self through the eyes of others, of measuring one's soul by the tape of a world that looks on in amused contempt and pity.

One ever feels his twoness, — an American, a Negro; two souls, two thoughts, two unreconciled strivings; two warring ideals in one dark body, whose dogged strength alone keeps it from being torn asunder. The history of the American Negro is the history of this strife, — this longing to attain self-conscious manhood, to merge his double self into a better and truer self. [62]

When we are faced with racial prejudice and hypocrisy from a hostile dominant society, and when social inequality and powerlessness come to define our lives, it can have a seriously adverse impact on what we come to believe ourselves to be.

Fulfilling the Stereotype

Think of what white people believe the stereotypical black man to be, the stereotypical black woman to be. Think of all the things we know white people and others have been taught or socialized to believe about us. Now think about what we truly are, what our parents and communities raised us to be. In the face of the media's onslaught, those of us without the tools to defend ourselves come to fulfill the roles the dominant culture tells us we must play. We can end up acting out self-denigrating behaviors by which we exploit one another for material gain, distorted admiration and an appearance of power. One of the ways that PTSS is reflected today can be seen in the recurrence of such stereotypical behavior. Take the role of the black male for example:

Black males were valuable to slave owners in a number of ways, the most obvious being their ability to perform arduous manual labor; another, however, was their breeding capability. These black males assured the continuance of human products that could be sold and trained in lifelong servitude. This role of 'breeder' was a sought-after position on the plantation because it offered special privileges like extra food or special jobs and power among the slave population. Today this role has morphed and reemerged to become the 'street hustler/womanizer' and the more contemporary 'gangster-pimp' replete with present-day material and social rewards. The audacious and flashy zoot suits of the 30's and 40's became the full-length furs, large brim hats and platform shoes of the 60's and 70's. Today we see oversized leather designer trousers and diamond stud earrings, while 'Hummers' and 'Bentley's' have replaced the highly prized Cadillac Eldorados and Lincoln Continentals of the past.

Entertainment provides other examples. Minstrels and vaudevillians set the stage for some of the first popularized stereotypic and racist images of black people. In the early 1900's, minstrel shows featured individuals both white and black in 'blackface,' idealizing slavery life by showing blacks as imbecilic and happy folks who adored their slave master. Slaves were portrayed as people who mostly sang and danced and cheerfully ate pig entrails and watermelon to pass the time. These shows were well-attended and were the first opportunity for blacks to perform on stage.

In the 1970's a new crop of exploitative performances surfaced. Black exploitation films like *Super Fly*, *Shaft*, *Trick Baby*, *The Mack* and *Sweet Sweetback's Baadasssss Song*, just to name a few, depicted black men as violent, criminal and oversexed; black women were depicted as docile and submissive, or as domineering and manipulative. In either case, women were portrayed as sex objects to be abused and controlled.

Some recent examples are films like *Training Day* and *Monsters' Ball* that bear a striking resemblance to the 'blaxploitation' films of the past. They differ only in that they are far more graphic and abysmal. There have been some constructive changes since the 70's in the film industry. However, there are still few roles for black actors where their versatility and skills as artists can be positively showcased.

In today's pop culture, young women and girls are casually referred to, and sometimes refer to themselves, as 'bitches' and 'ho's,' and engage in romanticizing social and cultural deviance. Music videos have managed to get done in a matter of minutes what full length films of yesteryear accomplished: namely, to provide the viewer with the immortal depiction of the black stereotype complete with drama, wardrobe 'bling bling,' sex and violence.

I remember seeing a television show that featured the homes and cars of famous wealthy individuals. One young black gentleman toured the audience through a sea of his 'stuff,' stopping at different junctures to elaborate about the fine details that made his possessions better than others. One of his stops was to show the viewers his numerous cars, including his favorite, a mink-lined Bentley. What was more outrageous than the car's vulgar excess was the fact that he was not yet even old enough to drive!

Vacant esteem, one manifestation of PTSS, can be seen in popular culture and contemporary television images of wealth. People who believe themselves to have little worth, little power, little self-efficacy, will often do whatever they can do to don the trappings of power, even if it means acting out the demeaning roles society considers appropriate for them. Others will try to deal with such lack of esteem by finding ways to 'neutralize' their pain with strategies that will enable them to turn that weakness into a sense of control. Elaine Pinderhughes in her book, *Understanding Race, Ethnicity, and Power: The Key to Efficacy on Clinical Practice*, describes one of those strategies:

> *Inspiring fear is another way of turning powerlessness into power. A Black psychologist made this point to a white colleague: My powerlessness as a Black male in the American system often leaves me with one sure way to get a sense of power – to scare you.* [63]

"Since you don't respect me, then you're gonna fear me!" These were the words expressed to me by a young man explaining why he expected white people to be afraid to drive through his neighborhood. He went on to say, "White people know that black people are left with the scraps, the remnants of a real society, and that since this 'scrap' is all that I have, I'm going to stand on it and protect it, stating: "You white people better be scared to come through here, 'cause I'm a dangerous black man."

In the same breath he laughed, saying how whenever he and his friends see white people driving through the 'hood' with their hands tightly gripping their steering wheels in fear, trying to avoid eye contact with them, they wait until the car moves out of sight to smile, shake their heads and laugh because they know that no one among them has the slightest intention of harming the terrified outsiders. From these black men's perspective, they were just protecting their 'turf.' What they don't understand is that standing by their principles through this game of intimidation could, and in many cases has, yielded harmful results for young men like themselves.

Arousing fear in others through intimidation and confrontation is a widely known tactic among African Americans. It is not surprising that it is a frequently employed theme of black comedians. In their 2000 performance, *The Original Kings of Comedy*, Cedric the Entertainer does a routine about the situation of someone coming late to a concert where they have pre-purchased their tickets for the show. He explains that the white person deeply '*hopes!*' that no one has taken their seats, whereas someone black (he says with great emphasis) '*wishes* someone WOULD try to take their seats.'

The implication here is that fear of conflict would lead white people to avoid, rather than confront the individual. The further inference is that black people are not afraid of conflict, and would not hesitate to confront the offender, regardless of their ethnicity. The truth underlying this behavior is: If we can't inspire positive qualities such as love, admiration or respect, at least we can inspire something.

Adaptations From Our Past

Unconsciously fulfilling the roles of the stereotypical hustler, pimp, 'ho,' thug, or dangerous black man are just some of the ways we can be impacted by Post Traumatic Slave Syndrome. I believe, that at the root of such role fulfillment is the issue of esteem. Vacant esteem is also a critical piece to the puzzle in many other manifestations of PTSS. It plays a role in our male/female relationships. It plays a role in our tendency to sabotage ourselves, in our inclination to shame one another, and in our propensity to compete against each other.

Black Male/Female Relationships

Why are there so many black single women raising their children? Where are all of the black eligible men? Why do so many black men seem to gravitate to white women, often to the total exclusion of black women? Why do so many black women suffer the brunt of black male hostility and violence?

These questions lay at the very crux of the challenges facing black male/female relationships, and comprehensive answers to them would fill the pages of an entire book. However, we can make a good beginning by first looking at some of the conditions which African Americans are currently confronting. According to the Bureau of Labor, the unemployment rate for African Americans is double that of whites and African American males continue to account for 50% of the prison population.[64] The toll that these two statistics alone have had on black families has been, and continues to be, dangerously underestimated. Chronic unemployment and disproportionate incarceration rates leave many African American families fragmented, powerless and all but incapable of stability.

Some would say, "But similar conditions have been experienced by every immigrant group to come to these shores and they were able to maintain their families and overcome. Today, Latinos and Asian immigrants face some of the same conditions as African Americans and they seem to be doing OK."

People, mostly white, have presented this argument to me dozens of times. They fail to take into account some very important factors. All of the groups that have held together started with strong family structures. They had long established the habit of family. When times got tough they relied more on each other. Often under stress they became even more unified.

Conversely, the history of blacks in America has been one of fragmentation. For more than 240 years slavery rendered black men and women impotent with regard to keeping their families together. Imagine the impact of generation after generation after generation of familial disintegration. What 'habits' do you think that produced? After emancipation African Americans began to build their families. Many of our ancestors had to start from scratch to develop the necessary skills to maintain a family, skills that so many people take for granted. Hopefully, in time these skills would become habits. To their credit, many did succeed. Many did not.

As with learning any new set of skills, stress impedes their development. Put a person under enough stress and he will revert to his old, ingrained, learned ways. So, when times got tough, as they did so often, many black families could not hold up under the strain and fragmented once again. It is a testament to our ancestors' strength, resilience and persistence that so many of them became, and so many of us have become strong husbands and wives, mothers and fathers. Unfortunately, many of us still have a long way to go.

Today, the white ideal of having a working male head of household earning a more than adequate income, and a stay at home mom who spends her days raising the children, baking cakes and planting flower bulbs, is rapidly becoming an unattainable luxury, even for white people. This sought-after picture, or whatever is the current picture of American success is turning into nothing more than a facade, a pretense of social and material achievement. African Americans have nonetheless bought into the counterfeit white image and struggle in vain to attain it.

With the ideal clearly out of reach, we eventually develop our own black facade of the white facade, playing out a pathetic attempt to arrive at what turns out to be a mere chimera. Falling short of what was never attainable, black men and women punish one another for not living up to the elaborately constructed fantasy. They then become reminders, one to the other, of their failure; they act as mirrors that reflect back what they come to believe stands between their losing or winning, their one immovable reality, their 'blackness.'

This punishment all too often comes in the forms of physical, emotional and psychological abuse black men and women visit upon each other in an ever intensifying cycle. Men physically abuse their female partners, who in turn emotionally and/or psychologically abuse them, which causes the physical abuse to increase, and so on. Please note that it is just as likely that women set this cycle in motion as men. Whether the man instigates this cycle or the woman, the end result is two damaged and hurting people, who once cared for one another, further damaging and hurting each other.

And if the physical abuse goes far enough, the lives of the women involved and the lives of their children can be seriously at risk. When this happens, what are their options? When they become victims in their own homes, black women are faced with yet another layer of oppression, together with the added collective internalized racism and historical trauma. They are not only punished relentlessly by the dominant society, whose legacy continues to threaten the lives of all of slavery's children, these women bear the additional brutal chastisement from black men. For their part, the men suffer from a kind of intra-psychic assault of demons emerging from a mythical masculine world of their own making, a world they create to endure their status of invisibility and impotence. He, in subduing her, begins to feel a hint of power that vanishes swifter than a shadow when he returns to his white male dominated world.

How long have these shadowy reflections haunted the relationships of black men and women? Is it possible that during slavery black men held resentments towards black women for not fighting against the master's sexual advances despite the fact that it was obviously out of her control? Did the black woman harbor contempt for the black man that did not protect her, even though she knew that any interference on his part could cost him his life? Still, they were – and we still are – human, with all of our human frailties. Yet the need for compassion has gainsaid any opportunities to adequately 'debrief' his or her experience then or now.

Rajen Persuad, in his book *Why Black Men Love White Women*, discusses the costs to male/female relationships of sexualizing the black woman and emasculating the black man. He further describes how the black woman was demoralized, in a word 'soiled,' and how the white woman came to be deified:

> . . .*The white woman was placed on a pedestal and even had normal biological functions performed for her. She was dressed in the finest clothes, sprayed with the most delightful fragrances and held up as a model of matriarchal supremacy. Her black counterpart served her from the bottom of the pedestal . . . .every inch of the black woman was used for toil without compensation. Her head to carry heavy loads, her breasts to feed white children, her hands to pick cotton, wash clothes, and till soil, her legs as transport through this torture, and her privates to pacify and pleasure her persecutors in order to preserve her people.* [65]

Persuad goes on to explain the impact of this deification, coupled with forbidden, access on the psyche of the black man.

> *The history and circumstance that has soiled the black woman's image has continued to direct the black man's mind away from that desperate*

sight toward that which he has longed to be recognized by. He sees himself as a historic failure – failing to provide for his family, protect his family and secure a livelihood. Additionally, he finds it difficult to connect with the black woman outside of sensation because she serves as a symbol of his systemic failure. [66]

The white woman can sometimes be utilized as a vacation from the black race. In its simple form, she is a break. A chance to forget everyday life . . . [67]

A black couple bears the same burdens that any other couple bears: finding gainful employment to support themselves; establishing a strong base from which to raise healthy children; carving out time to escape life's daily hassles and rekindle tender bonds of affection; time to simply 'do life' in the best possible way. They, however, have some additional baggage given to them by family long gone – old, dirty, and heavy baggage that needs to be repaired or discarded.

Nowadays it seems as though black couples are fighting to stay afloat. Like salmon, we battle against incredible odds to survive and to grow. Regardless of whoever it is we choose as mates to accompany us on our journey, anyone black will be swimming up stream.

Planning to Fail

It is not surprising, after decades of being depicted as ineffectual and inferior, that some might begin to believe that failure is inevitable. It is this expectation of failure that stops many youth from seeking college educations. It is this same expectation that can stop hard working adults from seeking promotions and advancing their careers. I can remember being told by my high school guidance counselor that I was not 'college material.' She was a middle-aged, embittered white woman that appeared to loathe the majority black population at Crenshaw High School, where she had served for far too many years as a student advisor. Unlike many of my classmates that may not have had a family history of success in higher education, I had role models that nurtured and guided me, so I was undeterred by her remarks. I was confident that I was, beyond the shadow of a doubt, 'college material.'

There were countless students like me who clearly had the ability to do well, but would often deliberately sabotage any chance they had for success by becoming chronically disruptive in class or ditching school altogether. When I pressed a friend to explain why she seemed to only act out so terribly when she was in school, she said that she didn't care at all about school, that nobody in her family went to college and there was no way she was going to make it either. I didn't think to ask her if she actually wanted to go to college, but I can understand how hard it must have been for her to believe herself capable without any examples within her immediate environment.

Some years ago I was a counselor in a summer program designed for African American children and youth. The primary focus of the program was to promote educational achievement. I remember Katrice, a young middle school student about thirteen years old, who was part of a career camp. When asked what careers might interest them, many of the young people responded with "I don't know;" others (males mostly) expressed their desires to go to the NBA; and a few wanted to be teachers. When the time came for Katrice to answer the question, she stated rather casually, "I want to be an engineer."

The gentleman who was leading the discussion responded with surprise and immediately asked the question, "How are you at math?"

It turned out that she had not only gotten straight A's in all of her math and science classes, she had pretty much received A's in all of her other classes as well. Her peers chuckled, at which point she became embarrassed.

Katrice expressed herself in a clear, articulate and confident way. She was extremely impressive and I was delighted to work with her. I ultimately became very involved with Katrice and her family, eventually becoming a mentor to her. In her sophomore year I met with her mother to discuss future college plans for Katrice. She was a devoted young woman working two jobs to support her three children, While her mother strongly desired for Katrice to attend college, she had no practical experience regarding how to assist her daughter in achieving her goal. She was a third generation teen parent and no one in those three generations had ever gone to college; few had even completed high school.

When I spoke with Katrice about attending college and asked her what schools she might be interested in, she could not imagine attending any school beyond the local community college that was within walking distance from her home. I explained that with her skills, if she kept her grades up, she could likely attend any university in the country. Still, she could not imagine living anywhere outside of her neighborhood.

Early during her junior year she began avoiding me. Her high school counselor contacted me because he had noticed that Katrice's grades were falling. After a few months I caught up with her at a basketball game. We spoke outside for quite a while. She explained how frightening it was to think of leaving her home and neighborhood to attend a school where she didn't know anyone. She also shared that her friends teased her about being a 'goody good' and accused her of trying to 'act white.' It was disturbing to me when I first heard that black youth experience peer pressure from one another to not achieve, and that getting good grades was equated with acting white. Now, unfortunately, such peer pressure has become commonplace.

It was apparent to me that Katrice wanted much more than she was letting on to those around her. I was able to help her see that going to college would not mean that she would be abandoning her family and friends; nor that doing well in school meant she was selling out. She once again became enthusiastic about the possibility of going on to college.

During Katrice's senior year, I was meeting with her mother to go over college applications and financial aid forms when I realized that her limited reading skills made it impossible for her to understand the materials in the application packet. I explained that the forms were difficult for everyone and that this was perhaps the most challenging aspect of getting into school. She laughed nervously and after a short time she began to feel more relaxed and comfortable. She shared with me how proud she was of Katrice and that she would do everything that she could to help her to be successful. I met with her nearly every day until we completed all of the paper work. I was able to get many of the application fees waived and was finally prepared to mail the application packages off when Katrice told me that she was pregnant and had decided that she no longer wanted to go to college.

Her mother was devastated, and as I spoke with her she avoided making any eye contact with me. I couldn't help feeling like I had pushed too hard, that my intrusion had caused Katrice to seek a desperate measure to escape a future that she feared. Perhaps I had inadvertently sentenced Katrice to follow the legacy of her family and some of her closest girlfriends, of dropping out of school and devoting her life to being a mother.

Katrice had a miscarriage, which left her ill for quite some time. She did eventually graduate from high school with high marks, but soon thereafter became pregnant again and embroiled in the fray of urban life. We kept in touch, though less frequently than before.

A year or so later I received a phone call from Katrice, now nineteen. She told me that she was moving to California with her son and that she had plans to attend a community college. She explained that she was unable to achieve any of her dreams while she remained in her neighborhood.

"They won't let me grow here. Whenever I reach for anything they begin to resent me and pull me down. I love them, but I have to go," she told me.

Katrice eventually completed her undergraduate education and became a math teacher. When last I heard from her she was pursuing an advanced degree. Katrice was one of the fortunate ones who stopped believing that failure was inevitable or acceptable. Unfortunately, there are numerous black youth that continue to believe that they are destined to fail, that success is reserved for those other than themselves, and that they lack what it takes to make it in this life.

Being told you are inferior for hundreds of years can have lasting psychic impacts, impacts that get passed from parent to child, to grandchild, to great grandchild. We know family traditions get passed down through generations. Fortunately for Katrice, she was eventually able to translate the strengths of her mother into meaningful achievement beyond raising a family.

Never Let Them See You Sweat: Escaping the Shame

I grew up knowing that you never air your 'dirty laundry;' to do so is tantamount to betrayal. I don't think that my experience was unique when it came to this hypersensitivity about maintaining closed boundaries about your personal life. Neither is this sensitivity limited to African Americans. To maintain appropriate levels of privacy when it comes to one's affairs is both appropriate and prudent. However, when privacy becomes secrecy and simple human imperfections are perceived as a cause for shame and humiliation, that is quite a different story.

This subject of shame is particularly significant when it comes to African Americans. It is as though people live with a constant fear of being exposed. I am not completely sure what exactly we are afraid of exposing. I only know that this fear is something a number of us live with, a collective knowing of sorts, the details about which have been long forgotten. This collective knowing can awaken from dormancy with a single insult, which in turn sends us reeling into attack mode in defense of our faltering pride. To publicly humiliate someone is an unspoken cultural taboo, yet shaming and humiliation are frequently employed in our attacks on one another.

This should not be confused with what is commonly referred to as 'playing the dozens,' a form of social 'roasting' with no intent to harm and that rarely results in hurt feelings and physical aggression.

What I am speaking of involves roasting with the deliberate intent to demoralize. When carried to excess this brand of 'roasting' can and often will lead to blows. Some time ago I was working in a neighborhood school with a majority of black students. Once in a while I was asked to supervise the two lunch periods. On one such occasion I was listening to a group of students talking with one another when the conversation became heated. Soon two young men were standing nose to nose yelling and swearing at each other. What I found strange about this and many similar squabbles that I had witnessed was what they chose to say during these fallouts, things like, "Your mama's on food stamps, that's why you got to get your clothes from the Goodwill."

It was words like these that led to blows and often, tears. So I took it upon myself to look up the records of the two students as well as those of a number of their companions that were observing the event. It turned out that all of them were on reduced lunch because their families were receiving public assistance, namely, food stamps.

It was some of these same young people that were embarrassed when I talked in their class about my trip to Africa. Seemingly with shame they asked me if Africans wore clothes and lived in houses. All that they had come to know, think and feel about one of the largest and culturally rich continents in the world was that they were ashamed of sharing a common ancestry with its inhabitants. I brought in pictures of Africans living in both modern and traditional homes, in villages and in cities, to provide them with a more accurate representation of African culture. I shared stories about the history, beauty and greatness of Africa along with the challenges and troubles facing it.

I explained that poverty, while one of the major problems facing most countries in Africa, including those in southern Africa where I visited, was not a source of embarrassment. The poor people living in the villages in Botswana and Lesotho were not humiliated by their poverty. On the contrary, they repeatedly reflected great dignity and self-pride despite their humble material possessions. The only indication of discomfiture expressed by those with whom I spoke was their lack of education. On many occasions individuals, usually adults, would tell us with enthusiasm that they were completing the equivalent of their high school education. They would then proudly assure us that their children would receive a better education than themselves.

In stark contrast, the African American youth were all ashamed about being poor and they punished each other for it daily. These early experiences with feeling ashamed no doubt lead to difficulties in adulthood. It would appear that the older the individual, the higher the stakes and the more elaborate the schemes devised to hide the shame.

It is this same sense of shame, together with a lack of healthy esteem that prompts African Americans to respond to news about a brutal rape or an armed robbery by anxiously asking if the perpetrator was black.

The men or women who drape themselves in gold and diamond necklaces and flaunt huge gaudy rings; who wear the most expensive shoes and clothes; as well as youth who dress in the most exclusive athletic wear or don designer hand bags, wear a picture of wealth. In the absence of wealth's authenticity, they use these to paint a picture of success to avoid the embarrassment they believe they will experience if the world knew their true circumstances. The façade wears thin in the face of living paycheck to paycheck, renting instead of owning, following instead of leading, and struggling to just keep the lights on.

I believe that this perpetual drama of finding ways to escape the shame is the end result of a people who have been robbed of any real knowledge of who they are and where they came from. It is a result of a people who have no understanding of how they arrived at where they now are and who are oblivious to the mechanisms by which their past has predestined their present. It is a result of a people who have been sold a bill of goods by America, the bill of goods that clothing, accessories, cars and all manner of material possessions define their worth. In truth, this bill of goods is a torrent of lies wrapped in a carefully manufactured advertisement, distributed and sold to them at a price far too exorbitant to measure.

Crabs in the Barrel

There is an old saying among African Americans that when someone black tries to pull themselves up in the world, 'like crabs in a barrel' another black person always reaches up to pull them back down. How often has the most unbearable antagonist at the job, at school, on the committee, in the church or mosque been another black person? No doubt fools and idiots come in all shapes, sizes and colors – and African Americans certainly have no shortage of them. However, there seems to be an uncanny tendency amongst many blacks to orchestrate and plot the demise of other blacks, sometimes even friends and relatives. It is as though the achievements of family and friends, colleagues and acquaintances are seen as a threat or an affront.

I don't believe that we can surmise this rather insidious form of jealousy to be an unfortunate cultural nuance and leave it at that. I think it bears closer scrutiny. I have noticed that layered between the resentment and envy are issues of fear or panic, coupled with feelings of abandonment and shame. There is a fear of being left behind by the very people who we have embraced as equals. The promotion of the black colleague is perceived as a betrayal more so than if the person who was advancing was white. We have been taught and socialized to believe that black people are at the lowest level of progress and achievement, that we are lazy, untrustworthy and criminal. So it follows reason that when someone black is promoted over another black person, the person left behind experiences a profound sense of inferiority.

If I believe that black people are inferior and someone who is black is being promoted over me, then I am lower than the lowest. If, on the other hand, someone white is promoted over me, again my socialization prepares me. I have learned to accept the white person being advanced as a normal process, be it fair or unfair. Historically, during slavery the promotion of one black person over another usually meant that they would soon use their newly acquired position to further tyrannize those blacks occupying lesser positions. Today, this is commonly referenced as 'overseer mentality,' where a black person in a position of power, often a manager, will act as a 'gatekeeper,' charged with making sure those of his or her race are kept in 'their place.' This individual also deters the people in charge from hiring or promoting anyone else who is black, thus removing any discomfort or perceived obligation on the part of the employer to hire more African Americans.

Taking on the negative stereotype as our identity; developing low expectations for ourselves, our families and our community; assuming that we will fail in most things that we set out to achieve; losing the critical respect for ourselves and thus diminishing others like us; perpetually trying to outrun the demon of shame by amassing material things in exchange for our dignity; forgetting how to love ourselves and each other: These are some of the ways the vacant esteem of Post Traumatic Slave Syndrome is manifested today. These stand out as some of the most serious, persistent and deleterious expressions of our culture's slave past.

A Matter of Respect

"Why are you all so angry?" This is a fairly common question posited by white people to African Americans. For a long time I was puzzled by statements white people made about how intimidating, aggressive, threatening, and intense black people as a group tend to be. I, of course, was included in their assessment and as such, endeavored to explore the question. While I don't consider myself particularly angry, I have on some occasions been described, and almost always by someone white, as being angry. I don't know if in general the average black person has more or less anger than Whites, Hispanics, Asians or any other group, or if whites simply have heightened feelings of guilt that contributes to this perception.

In truth, it matters little whether or not we are angrier than anyone else. What does matter is that a lot of us are angry, and there is a lot to be angry about. What matters even more is what we do with our anger. Before we look at ways our past has effected how we experience and express anger we first need to understand what often lies at the core of our angry feelings: Disrespect.

I began my research in 1990 with an investigation into the relationship between transgenerational traumas from slavery and the self-esteem of African Americans generations later. I wanted to know what black children were learning about who they were from other black people in their environment. I was surprised to hear some of the same self-deprecating comments being tossed around that I had heard as a child: negative assessments of skin color, hair texture and length, as well as intellectual capacity. As I began looking more closely I found that there were many historical links between these assessments and our slave past.

I entered a doctoral program in social work research where I continued looking at the connection between African Americans and historical trauma. The focus of my research was violence, whose precursor, anger, is one of the symptoms of Post Traumatic Slave Syndrome. I wanted to learn what impact certain conditions had on anger and violent behavior in African American male youth. The five conditions that I explored were: 1) being victimized; 2) witnessing violence; 3) dealing with daily urban hassles; 4) issues of respect; and 5) socialization. I surveyed 200 black teenagers between the ages of 14 and 18 as to the part each of these conditions played in their behavior. (Half were incarcerated, the other half were not.)

While the results of my investigation seemed to surprise many of my white colleagues, they were predictable to my black associates and myself. Being disrespected was as responsible for violent behavior as being the victim of, or witnessing violent acts. Being disrespected was more responsible than being the effect of the daily stressors that go with living in urban settings. I also found issues of respect to be the most significant antecedent in the expression of violence. One more time: The antecedent most likely to produce anger and violence in African American male youths is disrespect.

The other important result of this research is that positive racial socialization mitigates the feelings of anger that go along with being disrespected. So an African American man who has a strong sense of himself and his history is likely to be more resilient when he is disrespected and less likely to respond with anger and violence.*

Positive Racial Socialization

This socialization process teaches African American youth to understand the obstacles that are associated with being born black in the United States. When racial socialization is done correctly young people learn early on about the systemic racism that surrounds them, and they are taught the coping mechanisms and skills necessary to survive and thrive in such an environment. Through the guidance of family members and support from the community they learn that despite social barriers they are able to excel and prosper. Socialization occurs as families provide children with a historical and cultural map of the African American experience that describes how they have survived many adverse conditions beginning with slavery. The children learn how the belief in God and extended family has served to strengthen and insulate them from the negative effects of racism and discrimination. This will be discussed in much greater detail in the next chapter.

Disrespect

Being disrespected can be humiliating, frustrating and belittling. It is natural for a person to get angry at even one slight, let alone dozens, hundreds, even thousands. In the face of a multitude of assaults on personal dignity, it should surprise no one that violence may arise as a consequence.

As with most cultures, respect has always been an essential part of African and African American culture. The respect for adults and elders was demonstrated in numerous ways. One way was to acknowledge them first with a greeting upon entering a room or by addressing them by appropriate titles. During slavery Africans were not given titles of respect by whites. They were never addressed as "ladies" or "gentlemen," "Sir" or "Ma'am," 'Mister,' or 'Miss' or "Mrs.," so they conferred their own designation of respect. They addressed one another as "Big Mama," and "Big Daddy," "Ma-dea," "Sister" or "Brother" to convey honor. As a continuing legacy of slavery, African Americans today have recognized that the society around them does not always respect them and have developed a hypersensitivity to, and anger about being disrespected. This anger is manifested in a multitude of ways within the African American environment. Respect appears to be one of the linchpins in determining whether or not resolutions are arrived at aggressively or peaceably.

Today, slavery's children experience all manner of disrespect on a daily basis. We are disrespected at work, at the grocery store, at the mall, at school and at the bank. We are disrespected by the police, by doctors, by

---

* If you are interested in reviewing this research in detail please see: "A Dissertation on African American Male Youth Violence: 'Trying to kill the part of you that isn't loved." Portland State University. You may obtain a copy from the university or through my web site: www.joydegruy.com.

the media, by teachers, and by politicians. Perhaps most hurtful is when we are disrespected by our wives, husbands, children, parents, friends and peers. Of course this isn't new. Historically, we as a people have suffered the indignities of slavery, abuse and oppression for generations! It is no wonder we can be a little testy. And when a person lacks a strong positive sense of themselves, every incident can be perceived to be a personal attack.

A few years ago my daughter, a social worker, was working with tethered clients in Detroit. Tethered, meaning that her clients, who were under house arrest, wore anklets so that if they stepped outside the perimeter of their homes it would alert authorities that they had violated their probation. She called me one day crying, and told me, "Mom, something just happened to my client and I just can't deal with it. He killed somebody. He was almost out, just ready to be released and he killed somebody, mom."

She described how this young black male, 17 years old, had been caught selling drugs and was placed under house arrest. He was at home with his girlfriend, their baby and his mother when the drug dealer for whom he worked came by his house. The dealer demanded that the young man produce either the money or the drugs. The scenario unfolded something like this, as recounted by the youth's probation officer:

"Man, where's my money?," asked the dealer forcefully.

"You know I don't have your money. You know I got busted. That's how it is. That's how it goes. I don't have your money."

"Man you better give me my money right now!."

"I told you that I don't have the money, so do whatever you got to do," the young man responded defiantly.

The drug dealer got very angry, walked over to him and started to search his pockets.

"Hey man, whatever. You know, I don't have your money."

The drug dealer became angry, and started pacing back and forth, his rage building. Frustrated, he didn't know what to do. He started to walk towards the door and then he stopped, turned around, took a few steps toward the young man and said with all the venom he could muster, "You know what? You're a bitch! A sorry little bitch! And I just punked you in front of your girl, in front of your baby and your mama. You're just a punk-ass bitch."

After saying this, the drug dealer headed for the door, when the young man picked up a baseball bat, hurriedly approached the drug dealer, and beat him repeatedly until he was a sprawling red mass of limp flesh. The drug dealer now lay beaten to death in the doorway of the house and the future of the 17-year-old youth was sealed.

Interestingly enough, the black probation officer recounting the story to my daughter said, "They're probably going to try him as an adult and he's going to get the maximum penalty. But I can understand why he did it."

What was it that she (the black probation officer) understood? The truth is, what was actually exchanged was no more than harsh words. There was no real physical threat posed by the unarmed drug dealer towards the young man or his family. In fact, the drug dealer had turned to exit the house at the time of the attack.

I believe that what the probation officer and many more African Americans know about this situation is that those words uttered by the drug dealer struck at the core of the youth's fragile sense of self and manhood. It was as though he was being castrated and strangled all at the same time. The drug dealer had disrespected him in the presence of his family, something tantamount to shooting him in the heart. Public humiliation or disrespect is a cardinal sin; it is also an unfortunate fact of life for too many of us.

Perhaps a more important question is why did those words cut so deeply? Being the target of disrespect is lodged in our cultural consciousness. It is as if it were in our genes. We have come to expect it. Sometimes we feel it when no disrespect was intended. Sometimes we see it when it isn't even there. When a black person believes he or she has been disrespected, much more is actually at stake than meets the eyes of most people. What stands between a disrespected African American and the source of disrespect is almost four hundred years of history, four centuries of being the targets of humiliation and abuse. A history of racial conflict, inequality and contempt culminates in a moment that few people not of this culture could comprehend, let alone predict. Yet everyone black who has witnessed or heard of incidents like this understands the unspoken and ubiquitous cultural law that was operating – a law that bids a black man to draw the line over which another man dare not step. A demarcation line that shouts, "Not This Time! Not Today! Not Tomorrow! Not Ever Again!!"

Dealing With Disrespect: Manhood Under Attack

"You're a bitch! A sorry little bitch! And I just punked you in front of your girl, in front of your baby and your mama. You're just a punk-ass bitch."

These few words, these few utterances, these few sounds were enough to move a man to kill. What would you do? I bet some of you are thinking, "Damn straight! I would have gone after him too." I know many of you, even if you had restrained yourself from doing so, would certainly have felt like confronting the drug dealer. And, certainly, like the probation officer, if you are black you certainly understand why the boy lashed out.

My question is, how fragile does a person have to be to consider an insult an assault? Why do we so often hear, "His manhood was at stake. He had to do something."? Perhaps when we do not have sufficient self-esteem the idea of 'manhood' is all we have left. Perhaps when for centuries we have not been allowed to be 'men' our concept of 'manhood' has yet to mature. Perhaps our sense of who and what we are leads us to perceive any minor slight as an assault on our very core. And when our core is in danger we respond with anger, rage and sometimes violence. And this response often results in behaviors that undermine much of what we are working to accomplish.

My second son, Nadim, is in college. One day during his freshman year he came home quite angry. My friend and I asked him what was up.

He told us, "School is a joke. I don't have to put up with it. It's not worth the trouble."

When I asked him what happened he told me that his American History professor, a white man, was discussing how white people viewed African Americans in the early 20th Century. To highlight his point he put up a picture of white men in 'black face' and left it up in front of the room for much of the class. The class, in which Nadim was the only black man, laughed and joked about the picture. Nadim became angrier and angrier at the disrespect he felt from the professor as well as from his classmates.

This certainly wasn't the first time something like this happened; and it certainly will not be the last. Nadim spoke of other incidents involving this professor where the professor implied that blacks were inferior to whites in numerous ways. After talking with me and other family members Nadim calmed down and was able to see the event for what it was: another example of ignorance and racial insensitivity, at the least; and racism at most.

Imagine how many times something like this has happened? It may have even happened to you. A person is disrespected once too often at work so they blow up at their boss and lose their job. A person is disrespected at the hospital so they stop going to that facility. When they were younger they were disrespected over and over again by their teachers so they angrily decided education has no value.

As black Americans a number of issues and questions with regard to disrespect are in play: how likely are we to perceive someone's behavior or a situation as disrespectful; why do we perceive it as such; and how do we respond once we believe ourselves to be disrespected? Issues of respect and disrespect are central to the African American experience. A history as a people of hundreds of years of slavery, Jim Crow, the Klan, lynching, police brutality and the like would certainly have some influence on such perceptions. Add to this our personal experience of the injustice that runs throughout American society and it is no surprise that we are hypersensitive about matters of respect.

Let's consider this in terms of numbers. How many times in your life have you felt disrespected? How many times have you seen other African Americans disrespected? How many times have you heard about other African Americans being disrespected? I would guess that on the average, African Americans experiences of disrespect would far exceed those of the average white person. African Americans frequently have a visceral response to disrespect whenever it rears its ugly head. Even during times when the person being disrespected is not black, it is frequently the African American observer who will become vocal in support of the individual being maligned.

More significant than the number of times a person felt disrespected is the way they internalized the event; in other words, the emotional impact that the perceived disrespect had on them. In my experience African Americans tend to be more deeply affected by disrespect, a fact that causes them undue stress and difficulties.

Which brings us to the question of our response. In general, the more Post Traumatic Slave Syndrome impacts us the more likely we are to respond in a way that will ultimately not be in our best interest. Often these responses entail an emotional reaction to being disrespected. Though we may feel that our reaction is justified and appropriate at the time, the negative consequences of our reaction can outweigh the momentary sense of justice.

In the face of disrespect, whether real or perceived, African Americans must find a more workable way of dealing with it. We have little control over how others will behave, however, we have a choice as to how we respond and a responsibility to exercise that choice in a way that is useful. The ways in which we choose to respond influences the range of responses that our children come to believe are available to them. If we continue to be emotionally vulnerable to these acts of disrespect, we will relegate ourselves and our children to a life of victimization. At the very least we need to learn how to overcome our initial feelings and reactions, and respond in a way that serves us.

Brought Up To Be Brought Down

When you control a man's thinking you do not have to worry about his actions. You do not have to tell him not to stand here or go yonder. He will find his "proper place" and will stay in it. You do not need to send him to the back door. He will go without being told. In fact, if there is no back door, he will cut one for his special benefit. His Education makes it necessary. [68]

Carter G. Woodson

Since he was 12 years old my son attended predominantly white schools and had predominantly white friends. In 2004, at the age of 19, my son went to live with his grandmother in Detroit for six months. This would mark the first time in his life that he would live in a predominately black environment. Here he would gain first hand knowledge about what life is like for black people living in a large urban area. Our frequent phone conversations would reveal how deeply indoctrinated my son was with the images of black people that he had acquired from growing up in Portland.

I remember one conversation in particular that was unsettling to me. It was winter in Detroit and quite cold. My son was attending a nearby college and was working part-time at a grocery store. He met lots of black co-workers, male and female, young and old who helped him on the job and also gave him rides to and from work. He hated the actual work itself, but grew to enjoy being with the people with whom he worked.

From the moment he said hello I knew something was on his mind that troubled him. He was planning to leave Detroit in a few weeks and I thought maybe he was concerned about his finances. I was wrong. He told me he was calling because he was concerned for the people with whom he worked. He told me about a young woman in her twenties who was pregnant, working two jobs and having difficulty lifting the boxes the job required her to lift. He told me about the old black man who had been working at the grocery store for fifteen years who had never gotten a promotion. My son told me how he would often stand up for the old man when the gentleman was being ordered around by a twenty-year-old white manager who humiliated him by speaking to him as though he were a child. Then there was the woman in her sixties, one of many co-workers that would give him a ride to work each day. He described how she never listened to the radio but instead played religious tapes and sang gospel music. She also refused to take any money from him in return for driving him to work.

My son shared with me that he hated leaving them. They were kind and hard working people who encouraged and helped him. They never asked for anything other than friendship and rarely had a complaint or unkind word to say about anyone. He spoke as if shocked by how deeply spiritual and caring these individuals were, and how diligently they performed their work.

"These were good people," he said, sounding surprised. "Most everyone I met was friendly and fun to be around." I inquired as to why he seemed so surprised. He said, "At first I was confused about why I expected something less of them. Then he told me he felt shame and outrage about what he had learned growing up in Portland.

He was becoming aware that he had bought into the headlines, the hype and the images the white community sells about black people. He was angry that he had been misled. In a word, he, like so many others like him, was unwittingly indoctrinated into racist socialization. Too many of us still are affected by the lies this society has attempted to foist upon us since its inception, lies that people in this society still spread to perhaps assuage their guilt and justify their crimes.

I recently asked a group of African American youth to join my class of graduate social work students at Portland State University in a discussion about two recent police shooting deaths in Portland, one involving an African American man and the other an African American woman, both of whom were unarmed.

The 15 young men and women, ranging from 14 to 20 years old, were reticent at first to speak openly and honestly. One of them found it difficult to mention the term 'white' because all but about three of the college students in the room were white.

Before the discussion everyone viewed a video of a taped interview with the young spoken word hip hop artist Malik Yusef. Malik talked about his life growing up on the South-side of Chicago and his experience being poor, angry and frustrated. He related how his poetry provided him with a vehicle for transcending the family and community troubles which surrounded him. Malik spoke openly and honestly about growing up in a tough neighborhood. He spoke about why he engaged in criminal behavior and his experience with police officers. The video was a great icebreaker. It opened up the youth to talk about their experiences and feelings regarding their own encounters with police. Much of what was shared involved the typical harassment of being stopped and searched for no reason, or being questioned about why they were in a park or walking home at night. Perhaps the most significant words they shared were their sentiments concerning the media's coverage of the events that occurred in their communities, communities which are largely Black, Hispanic and poor.

One of the youth, a young 19 year-old woman, reminded the class of the shooting months earlier of a young child. She told the class that she was one of the first people to arrive on the scene and that she had held the head of the wounded child for 45 minutes before paramedics arrived.

"Nobody shared that story on the news, how I held that kid's head until help came. They report every drive-by or robbery or assault that someone young and black commits, but they never show the good things that we do. Why is that?"

The last to share was a young woman who had remained silent throughout the entire discussion. When she finally raised her hand to speak, the rest of the youth immediately became quiet, as if anticipating something weighty. Her t-shirt sleeves were rolled up over her shoulders and several elaborate tattoos were visible. She spoke clearly and deliberately giving full eye contact to my class of graduate students. She shared how she had been watching the news, watching various people being interviewed about the fatal shooting death of James Jahar Perez, the unarmed black man I spoke of in chapter three. She recounted hearing a black woman, who, while being interviewed said, "It was wrong the way the police shot and killed Mr. Perez. The man didn't have a weapon."

"Next," the student went on, "a white woman was interviewed." The student slowly dropped her head and began to sob loudly,. "The white woman . . . the white woman said that the police were right."

There was an uncomfortable silence as she wept. The director that had accompanied these youth gently placed his arm on her shoulder. Quite unexpectedly the young woman tearfully raised up her head, turned to my students and asked, "When are you going to get it? Black people are struggling everyday to just barely live, how long do we have to go through this? What will it take for you all to just let us live?"

A hush fell over the class and the young woman gathered herself and sat back in her chair. Later many of my students shared that they were fighting back tears themselves, not because they felt any responsibility or guilt, but because of the desperation, rawness and truth of her words. She spoke to them almost as if she had hopes that it would somehow make a difference, that only they, as white students, could possibly change things.

From my perspective this was testimony to a greater truth: that she and her peers still held the belief that real power only rests in 'whiteness' and that in this acknowledgment these youths see themselves as powerless.

When African Americans accept the deprecating accounts and images portrayed by the media, literature, music and the arts as a true mirror of themselves, we are actually allowing ourselves to be socialized by a racist society. Evidence of racist socialization can be readily seen when African American children limit their aspirations, seeking out careers as nurses and paralegals rather than as doctors and lawyers. It can be seen when we use the accumulation of material things as the measure of self-worth and success. Racist socialization is evident in our failure to support our communities economically; in believing that the ice in the white man's store is somehow colder; in deifying whiteness and denouncing everything that is black. The ultimate result of this socialization is that all that is white becomes synonymous with power and that which is black is equated with impotence.

Society, its laws, educational systems, and propaganda are powerful forces, forces that can, and often do, have much greater impact than parents, extended family, peers, and even community. So, in spite of all our forebears who worked to survive and gain their freedom; in spite of our ancestors' efforts to build lives for themselves and their heirs; in spite of the efforts of all those who fought for our civil rights; in spite of all our parents did to support, educate and encourage us; in spite of all we do and have done to grow ourselves and raise our children, far, far too many of our people are still believing the lies. We are continually being socialized by this society to undervalue ourselves, to undermine our own efforts and ultimately to hate ourselves. We are raising our children only to watch America tear them down. And for some of us it's worse yet. It is as if we are still doing the work of those that enslaved us, for in believing and propagating their lies we keep ourselves and our children chained to the dominant culture's vision.

Today the legacy of slavery and oppression remains etched in our souls. The impacts of our history can be witnessed daily in our struggle to understand who and what we are, and in our jaundiced vision of who and what we can become. The impacts of our history can be witnessed in our continual fight for respect, respect that we seek and demand from without, but that can only be built from within. These impacts can be witnessed in the war between affirmative racial socialization in our homes and destructive racist socialization everywhere else, a war that I'm sorry to say, we seem to be losing.

While many of us have overcome, raised healthy families and achieved success, many of us still struggle with issues of esteem, anger and respect. Many of us are continually working to define who and what we are in relation to each other. Not enough of us are truly at peace with ourselves and our place in the world. Not enough of us have truly happy, thriving families. And what about those who have not achieved even the outward trappings of success? Many more African Americans live towards the bottom of the socio-economic ladder than live at the middle, and fewer still live towards the top. The great majority of us are struggling to provide for our families, keep them safe and growing in positive directions. In this respect we seem to be no different from the vast majority of Americans. Yet we are different. The difference is that we are working to do all this under the added weight of vacant esteem, ever present anger and racist socialization, the legacies of our past.

Whether or not we have overcome, most of us have been impacted by Post Traumatic Slave Syndrome in one way or another. Actually, many white people have been also, but that's the topic for another book. Understanding the role our past plays in our present attitudes, outlooks, mindsets and circumstances is important if we are to free ourselves from the spiritual, mental and emotional shackles that bind us today, shackles that limit what we believe we can be, do and have. Understanding the part Post Traumatic Slave Syndrome plays in our evolution may be the key that helps to set us on the path to well-being.

Chapter 6:

Healing

I often speak about my trip to South Africa where I traveled with
eight other African American women throughout several countries in
the southern region of Africa. It was a very intense six week journey.
Our goal was to establish an ongoing relationship with African women,
build a corridor that black women from both continents could use
to share cultures, and improve our collective lives. This experience
deeply affected me emotionally, so I tended to cry a lot. In fact, I cried
so frequently that the women traveling with me got a little perturbed.
They became disconcerted because every time I would cry, the South
Africans would simultaneously begin singing. Nobody attempted to

stop me or hand me a tissue; they would just sing. This was simply startling for my group at first but soon the real issue emerged. After they finished singing extemporaneously in four part harmony, they would turn to the women in our group and ask us to offer up a song or two. Herein lay the problem the other eight women in my group began to have with my crying all of the time. Nonetheless, we all became 'singers' over those six weeks.

The evening before we were scheduled to travel to Lesotho my eight companions, who included my sister and niece, sat me down to discuss the singing and crying issue. It kind of seemed like an intervention. My sister, speaking for the group, began, "Joy, as you know, we're going to Lesotho. . .and Joy . . . we're not singing! So, whatever you have to do to get yourself together, get it together, because we're not singing in Lesotho."

I apologized for being so emotional and promised to keep it together during our visit. The next day we arrived at the home of a family who were our hosts just in time for a reception dinner in our honor. People came from numerous towns and villages. Their were several translators who translated what we shared with the group into several different languages. This is the way it worked: each of us would stand up, introduce ourselves and tell a little about why we had come. Then the translator would translate what was said.

I was the first to introduce myself. I stood up and said, "My name is Joy, I'm from Portland and I'm traveling with eight other African American women. We're are hoping to build and sustain a positive sharing relationship with our African sisters. I am very happy to be here." I then sat down.

The translator began translating what I had said and the nine of us noticed that despite the brevity of my comments, the translator seemed to be going on and on at length. Soon the people in the room started to chant, and then they started to clap.

My sister gave me a puzzled look as if to ask, 'Is this going to happen after every introduction?' I leaned over to the translator and whispered as inconspicuously as I could, "I know that I didn't say very much, so what exactly did you say to them?"

He said, "I told them exactly what you said, but when I got to the point where I said that you were African American women, I needed to explain what that meant. You see, many of the people in the audience are from small, isolated villages with limited exposure to outsiders and they thought that all Americans were white. So, I had to explain to them that the eight of you were the descendents of the ones who had been stolen away. They were chanting back to you, 'Welcome home.'

Once again everyone began singing, because I had burst into tears. I caught a glimpse of my sister glaring at me and shaking her head because she knew that once again, we would all have to sing.

As I wiped the tears from my face, I had noticed a woman standing in the back of the room watching me, now she began walking over to me. She shared that she had studied for many years in the United States, then gently took me by the hand, and said,

"Did you think that we would forget you? I am from Lesotho, Lesotho is my home. If I leave Lesotho, Lesotho is still my home. If I leave Lesotho for fifty years, Lesotho is still my home. You are African, 300 years from home. We mourned Martin and Malcolm with you, we are so proud of you, we just wondered when you were coming home." The tears flowed and we sang yet again!

So what became of us, the prodigal children, since leaving home? We experienced the appalling cruelty of being stripped from our native land, and being torn from our families and endured the tortuous journey of the *'middle passage'* . . . and we still rose. We were divested of our language, culture and customs, bought and sold like livestock, raped and bred to perpetuate more victims, crushed beneath more than two centuries of government-sanctioned tyranny . . . and we still rose. We were made to labor a lifetime for another with no recompense, only to be released to suffer even more from the indignities of the Black Codes, Convict Leasing, Peonage and Jim Crow . . . and we still rose. Thousands upon thousands of us continued to be brutalized, marginalized, tortured and lynched . . . and still we rose. How is it that a people who suffer generation upon generation from abuses such as these and more still manage to rise!

Yes, we have still managed to rise. In spite of our past we have still made strides. We are a people of uncommon strength and fortitude. Our growth though, has been slow and stunted. Three steps forward, two steps back. We know there is still so much more we have to do, yet today we are rapidly approaching an impasse. The world is changing and we are lagging behind in our preparation to take advantage of the new order. In many ways we are becoming less educated, not more. In many ways we are becoming less conscious, not more. In many ways we are becoming less spiritual, not more. While greater opportunities are available for a select few, far fewer opportunities are available for the many.

In the future, if we are to move ahead and thrive we need to truly understand and accept who we are as a people. It is through knowing who and what we are that we can identify our strengths and build upon them. Then, using our strengths, we need to heal from the injuries of our history. We need to heal ourselves. We need to heal our families. We need to heal our communities. Once we know ourselves and are solidly on the path to health, we can move at the pace necessary to more than catch up: we can excel.

Knowing Ourselves

So who and what are we? If we are to believe what the dominant society would seemingly like us to believe, the lies they promulgate: we are stupid, criminal, unmotivated, lazy, underachieving, immoral and undisciplined . . . in a word, inferior. History reveals a very, very different story.

African Americans are a strong people, a seemingly infinitely resilient people. We have a long, long history of enduring and persevering through the severest of trials. Our ancestors endured slavery and persevered through Jim Crow. Evidence of these qualities can be seen today through our struggle for civil rights and our continuing pursuit of a level playing field.

We are an industrious people. We have built communities under seemingly impossible circumstances. During the Great Depression when the entire country was under enormous duress, we managed to care for one another with fewer resources than even the poorest of whites. Families gathered together, usually in churches, to help sustain large numbers of blacks and see them through those extremely tough times.

We are a creative people. Through slave times and the oppressive decades that followed we established a distinctive culture replete with new language, names, customs and behaviors. We have invented our own games, foods, music, art and fashions. Many of us have managed to carve out a prosperous existence from what at times amounted to society's scraps.

We are a just and forgiving people. Think about it. Despite the relentless oppression under which blacks have lived since slavery, there has been no large scale, organized, retaliatory 'terrorism' fueled by hatred and a need for revenge. We have demonstrated time and again that while we can courageously fight for justice, we are not crippled with hatred and rage, proving ourselves to be among the most magnanimous of people.

We are a spiritual, loving and hopeful people. It is amazing to me, that after all the work done to dominate, diminish and destroy us, after centuries of the most vile and horrific abuses meant to break our spirit and will, that we still have faith in God. It is a tribute to our fundamental decency that we still have a love for humanity. It is a testament to our fortitude that we still can hope and dream.

These are some of the components of our true nature. We, as a people, seem to have forgotten that this is who and what we are. We seem to have forgotten our own nobility. We have forgotten our own greatness. Perhaps many of us have never known! This is not surprising given all the time, money and energy spent over centuries to convince us to accept the degraded status imposed upon us. Whatever the case, it is vital that we collectively regain this knowledge so we can take our rightful place in the world community. It is crucial that we come to understand ourselves and have that understanding permeate us to our very core, for such a deep understanding will make healing from our wounds that much more complete.

Healing from Injuries Past

Certainly we need to heal from our historical injuries, and we need to do more. We need to become healthy. Healing will take us only part of the way. Working towards heath and well-being will take us to our goal. It is important that we discuss this distinction. There is a significant difference between not being sick and being well. If we are to heal and become healthy we will do so by building upon our strengths. We will need to draw upon our inner fortitude, resilience and endurance. We will need to tap into our industriousness and creativity. We will need to avail ourselves of our innate sense of justice as well as our proclivity for acceptance. Most of all we have to apply our spirituality and ability to love to the task before us.

How do we do this? I certainly don't have all the answers. I suspect no one person does. But I believe I have a few with which to begin. Completing our work will take more thought, research and insight, and we will need contributions from many within and outside of our community.

In Chapter 4 we discussed the three primary patterns of behavior associated with Post Traumatic Slave Syndrome: vacant esteem, ever present anger and racist socialization. In Chapter 5 we examined some of their manifestations in our culture today. It is now time to consider establishing new, healthier patterns of behavior, patterns that will be the foundation upon which a new and powerful legacy can develop. Rather than crush self-esteem, we must do everything in our power to build it. Rather than be torn down by the anger that is present within us, we must be able to create and maintain a state of inner well-being. Rather than allowing our children to be socialized by a racist society, we must consciously and deliberately educate and socialize them to understand their inherent nobility.

This all would seem a lot easier said than done. Surely there is much work to do. The primary question is will we do what it takes? Will we take the time to foster greater health for ourselves, families and communities? In part the answer to these questions will strongly be influenced by what we believe about our worth and efficacy.

Building Self-Esteem

Beliefs are powerful! Remember our discussion in Chapter 4? They strongly influence how we think, feel and behave. And their influence can be negative or positive. If a person has negative beliefs about their value and skills, they will often self-sabotage their efforts or cease trying at all. If a person has a positive belief about their ability and worth, they are more likely to achieve the results they are after. When we believe ourselves to be unworthy or incapable these beliefs have little basis in fact, yet they can still be powerful influences. What we need most in these instances is evidence to the contrary. If we can see that we are, in fact, valuable, that we are, in fact able, we will change our beliefs about ourselves accordingly.

So far we have talked about vacant esteem and some of the ways in which it manifests itself in our lives today. If we are to heal, one step we must take is to ensure we build our own self-esteem as well as the self-esteem of our children. For many this will be no easy task; our esteem has been buffeted by the storms of slavery, oppression and marketing for so long. For some, building up their esteem may take years, and some families may even take generations for their esteem to stabilize. Rarely have those who have suggested it known how to achieve it – to the frustration of us all. All this being said, please know that it certainly can be done. Mostly it takes perseverance and patience, (two of our great strengths, by the way). Actually, building self-esteem can be a very straightforward exercise.

Building esteem can be expedited if we understand its components. If you remember, esteem means worth or value. Self-esteem has to do with our evaluations of our own personal worth or value. To have a good assessment of our worth requires two simple building blocks: first we have to, in fact, be valuable and second, we have to be aware of the value we produce.

Hence, here is the question that is at the core of our esteem: Are you destroying or creating? This is the essence of esteem. Have you discovered your unique gift and shared it with others? Do things get worse or do they improve around you? Are others' lives poorer or richer because you are alive? Do you make the world a better place? When people leave your company do they feel better than before you arrived? These are some of the signs of value. Did you provide for your children today? Did you do good work at your job? Did you do the best you could do in school today? Did you make someone smile?

These are some of the most important questions to ask ourselves —yet so few of us do. These are key questions about the value that we produce. We all know people who often leave us feeling more bothered, confused, fearful or sad after we spend time with them. These people tend to express negative value. At the extreme negative end of the value scale, there are some people who seem to make us less able, weaker, less energetic. They are like vampires – you know, they suck the life out of us. Then there are others, those special people in our lives who generally leave us feeling happier, brighter and healthier. These people express substantial positive value. At the positive end of the value scale, some of them help you become more able, stronger, and more alive. They are extremely valuable individuals.

We all need to honestly and accurately evaluate ourselves, our actions and the consequences we produce. This is especially important for those who hold positions of leadership or are otherwise in the public eye. For example, if you are an artist, for instance a musician, does your music reinforce demeaning stereotypes and debase people? Or does your music inspire and ennoble people? Does your work promote unconsciousness or awareness?

And this brings us to the second building block of self-esteem: awareness of the value we produce. Most of us do things of great value every day, and we simply aren't aware of them. We spend way too much time focusing on the negative and take the positive for granted. When we are evaluated in school or at work if we receive 23 positive remarks and 2 negative ones, we tend to focus on the two negatives. Some years ago during an interview the champion golfer Tiger Woods was asked if he learned from his mistakes. His response surprised most of his audience. He answered by saying that he never pays attention to what he did wrong. Instead he said he focuses on what he did right and works to improve those things.

How many of us work in jobs we consider mundane and relatively meaningless, never considering all the good we're actually doing? Whether we are blue collar workers or white, work for minimum wage or for the big bucks, rarely do we pay attention to all those we are truly helping. The administrative assistant to a claims adjuster at an insurance company is one of a long line of folks that help others recover from their losses. That assistant contributes to making people's lives whole again on a daily basis. The important question is, are they aware of all those that they impact? And we haven't even spoken about all the good they do providing for their family.

In 1994 my friend's father was dying. He had only a few months to live when my friend wrote his father a letter. In the letter he thanked his father for all that he had done to raise him and help make him the man he had become. My friend also pointed out what he thought were some of his father's most significant accomplishments: raising three strong sons, all of whom became good, honest men; being a wonderful, supportive husband for 45 years; and being one of the kindest, most gentle of men who helped everyone he could. He made others laugh and feel welcomed.

My friend's mother told him that upon reading his letter, his father cried for a very long time. You see, his father thought his life was a failure. He never forgave himself for the failure of his first marriage. He believed he never provided enough for his wife and sons. He never believed he did enough. He rarely, if ever, paid attention to all the good he did and all the people he touched. I hope that by the end he understood.

In African American culture there is no lack of pride in the accomplishments of our family members and friends; however, there is frequently a paucity of personal, one-on-one acknowledgment of their deeds. I have often heard parents praise other members of their family once they have left the room, as if to praise them in their presence would be improper. In the absence of voiced recognition and praise from their elders, children often feel like their parents are not proud of them and carry a lifetime of self-doubt as to their worth. Healthy esteem comes from healthy and positive exchanges with the people in our lives on whom we depend for support and guidance.

Some families take time to consider all that went well for them the previous day, explore ways of making things even better, and plan what will go well the next day. Imagine every black family doing this every day. It wouldn't take long for you and your children to get in the habit of paying attention to the impact all of us have on others, and refining the impacts of our contributions. Every day we would have evidence of the good that we do, and hence evidence of our value. Where we are harboring beliefs that undermine our esteem, attending to the positive impacts we have will begin to destroy such limiting and fallacious beliefs. Creating value on a daily basis will provide strong, incontrovertible evidence of our efficacy and worth.

False and negative beliefs about esteem and efficacy are some of the issues confronting many of us. In the African American community there are many other false and negative beliefs that we leave unexamined. Beliefs about helplessness, beliefs about mainstream society, beliefs about victimization and many others that serve to put limits on what we can be, do and have. To address these falsehoods we need to look at ourselves and our community as a whole from a strengths rather than from a deficit perspective. We need to identify, focus and articulate those positive characteristics in all of our interactions with our neighbors, co-workers family and friends. And we need to especially share these encouraging observations with African American children whose views of themselves are still being shaped.

Taking Control of Our Inner World

The anger that lies just below our awareness and at times bursts forth, seemingly out of our control, is real. There is much to be angry about. Many of us have accepted these feelings as simply the way we are. This anger contributes to a shortened life-span. This is not just simply 'the way we are.' To some degree this anger is killing us. In some ways it's like a pain we've adapted to and accepted. Unfortunately, as we adapt and accept we don't see the need to handle our anger and reduce our stress.

When human beings have been exposed to stress early on in their lives, that stress can have profound effects on their ability to manage and control their emotions as they get older. Doctors have actually found a 'stress hormone,' cortisol, a chemical in our bodies that clouds our ability to be rational. For many people the effects of this stress hormone begin before they are even born. Recent studies have revealed that pregnant women can pass cortisol through the placenta to the infant, the impact of which can be devastating. After birth the continual exposure to stress releases more cortisol into the bloodstream, preventing the neural connections necessary to access higher brain functioning. And this release of higher levels of cortisol could result in limited learning ability.

Under stress, with our higher brain functions inhibited by cortisol, our lower brain functions take over and 'fight or flight' survival behaviors become prominent. When these lower functions are in play, children as well as adults begin to live as though every stressful event is a threat; which in turn causes the release of more cortisol, further inhibiting access to the reasoning parts of their brain. You can probably recall instances where you have witnessed individuals faced with a simple directive who respond as though they are under attack. Once stressed, the individual must return to a calm and balanced state in order to access their ability to reason. Some people can live in a constant state of crisis, becoming, in a way, addicted to the stress and finding ways to trigger the release of cortisol and live in a perpetual cycle of conflict.

The good news is we can take measures to mitigate our anger, reduce our stress, and feel more at ease and at peace. We can take measures to gain greater control of ourselves and the way we respond to our world. This too, is part of healing.

Given that much of the anger that we often feel is a direct result of being wronged, we need to find effective ways to address the mistreatment that will make things right. Our response to unjust treatment naturally arouses feelings of frustration, and it is at these times that we often let our anger get the best of us. Instead of determining how to right the wrong we respond angrily, which neither helps us attain what is rightfully ours, nor alleviates the feelings stirred up by this event.

For example, imagine being shorted hours on your paycheck. There is no benefit in becoming angry, yelling at the clerk who delivered your check to you, and storming out of the building. After all, the clerk had nothing to do with the mistake and leaving the building in a rage won't get you the money that you're owed. If you were to find yourself in this situation, what are some of the workable options available to you?

Whatever the case, regardless of whether what is occurring is blatant racism, a personality conflict, or just a simple accounting error, you must retain a level of composure which allows you to make rational decisions. It is impossible to make sound decisions while simultaneously being enraged. For many this sounds like common sense, but for those that have few tools other than anger or aggression to confront the injustices imposed upon them, this is no easy task. So, first, if you're angry wait for your anger to subside, which may require you to remove yourself from the situation for a while. Remember it is almost impossible to think rationally when you are angry. Find a way to wait until you become calm. Once you've calmed down, you can plan your response and more often than not you will find you have many options.

Probably the most obvious option would be to first determine the source of the error and begin the process of correcting the matter. If the problem occurred because there has been a simple accounting error you might have an easy time fixing the trouble. If your manager has deliberately docked your hours ask him for a written explanation, then produce in writing evidence that supports your argument. If you still cannot solve the problem, follow the proper grievance procedures and consider finding better employment.

Another option is to get someone that you trust as an advocate with whom you can discuss the issue. Many people find it difficult to articulate their concerns under tense conditions and find it helpful to talk over the situation with a friend before dealing with the event. Sometimes you can get someone to act as an intermediary.

Yet another option is to determine whether this particular offense warrants your time and attention at all. In other words, choose your battles. In many instances we are much better served by simply moving on and focusing our attention on things that will be of greater benefit to us in the long run. This usually requires that we have a 'Plan B.' I am a strong advocate of having a back-up plan, especially as it relates to our income and livelihood. When we have such a plan, we have options, and options give us a sense of freedom and peace of mind.

Stress takes a toll on our minds and bodies. Stress can make us feel fatigued, irritable, depressed and even ill. When we experience too much of it we can feel like our lives are not under our control. Conversely when we feel like we're in control of our lives we are healthier mentally and physically.

We are forever hearing about the benefits of regular exercise and healthy eating. We are encouraged to walk, run, bike, swim, do yoga and stretch. We are told to eat fewer foods with sugar and fat, and more foods high in fiber. We hear about it so much, it's as if that's all we have to do to live happy, fulfilling lives. While it is obviously simplistic to believe diet and exercise will cure all that ails us, it is true that they can have an inoculating effect when we are emotionally assaulted. They can help us maintain our balance, and the more balance we have in our lives, the less likely we will be to react emotionally, and the longer we can remain calm.

Beyond exercise and diet, anything we can do to make our lives easier would be great. Doing our best to take more time for ourselves and families is always a good idea. Another important step we can take to make our lives easier is to manage our finances in a way that creates stability and wealth. More and more Americans are living with greater and greater debt, and with increased debt comes increased stress. In the face of all the energy advertisers are directing at us to buy their stuff, we have to make sure we do not succumb to their efforts to turn us into mindless consumers.

Historically African Americans have had to deal with issues of severe poverty. Again and again we have demonstrated the capacity to live and function within our means, even during times of overt discrimination and in the face of limited resources. Now, the quest for material possessions has lead to frivolous spending and shortsighted financial planning, perpetuating the cycle of inherited debt instead of bequeathing to our children the fruits of our labors. Learning to make sound financial decisions will insure our children's futures, as well as increase our own well-being.

Racial Socialization

Americans are socialized to believe in the American dream. They are socialized to believe that America is the land of opportunity: a land in which anyone can, with hard work and ingenuity, accomplish anything; a land in which even a person from the poorest of backgrounds can one day grow up to be President. They are socialized to believe they live in a country in which the ideals of equality, liberty and justice for all reign supreme. They are socialized to believe America is the best country in the world and that Americans are the best people. Most Americans believe themselves to be the most caring, most just, most industrious and most generous people in the world.

And most Americans are socialized to believe that white is better. It's better than yellow; it's better than red; it's better than light brown and it's much better than dark brown. The poorest, most ignorant, ill-tempered white person still believes themselves to be better than anyone not white.

This was brought home to me in Andrew Hacker's book *Two Nations: Black and White, Separate, Hostile, Unequal.* In his book Dr. Hacker tells of a parable he presents to his classes. He asks his students to imagine they are visited by an official they never have met. The official proceeds to tell them the organization he represents has made a mistake. According to their records all of them were supposed to be black, and the rules being what they are, this mistake needs to be fixed immediately, so tomorrow all of them will wake up black. He tells them they will remain the same people inside, with the same thoughts, knowledge, and ideas, but they will have all the features of men and women of African American descent. No one they know will recognize them.

The official emphasizes that being born to the wrong parents is in no way the fault of the students, and that his organizations is prepared to offer some reasonable recompense. Would you, the official asks, care to name a sum of money you might consider appropriate? He lets them know the organization can be quite generous, and finishes by saying that their records show they are to live about another fifty years.

When this parable has been put to white students, most seem to feel it would not be out of place to ask for $50 million, or $1 million for each coming black year. And this calculation conveys as well as anything, the value white people place on there own skins. [69]

When he asks his students how they arrived at their figure, most respond by listing the discriminations they will almost certainly experience as a consequence of their black skin and features. Most are unaware that they are putting a value on their whiteness and devaluing blackness. I suspect that many white people placed in the same situation would feel the same in their heart of hearts.

We, as African Americans are also affected by this racist socialization. Many of us behave as though we believe that white is somehow better, that we are the deficient people that white people say we are. This is one of the most insidious consequences of Post Traumatic Slave Syndrome. At the same time many of us also believe in the illusion of the American dream. Becoming clear about who we are as well as what is needed for our material and spiritual success is the foundation upon which our health depends. We need to tell our children the truth and prepare them to thrive in the real America. We need to replace America's racist socialization with racial socialization.

Racial socialization is the process whereby we come to know our strengths, understand the world in which we live, and position ourselves to thrive. Continual education is at the heart of racial socialization. For young children, education is the elders' responsibility. For us adults, the responsibility is our own. We have to remain vigilant and questioning. We have to constantly endeavor to keep ourselves informed and our education current. We have to question the images we ourselves are portraying. We have to examine the sounds and pictures we expose ourselves to. We have to filter what we hear on the news and strive to understand what is true.

Telling The Truth About The World

There is no single prescription for protecting people against racism, bigotry and hatred; there is no one-shot inoculation against intolerance or fanaticism. However, it appears that educating people to understand that these things do exist, and about the manner in which they are manifested, can be helpful to those who come face to face with them. Racial socialization can be a process whereby individuals are taught how to identify and deflect the potential negative effects of assaults, overt as well as covert. These assaults may come in the form of individual diminishment, such as blatant name calling or condescension, or may be targeted at African Americans in general. For example, In 2001, the headline of a local Georgia newspaper read:

NO INTELLIGENT BLACK MEN FOUND HERE

The article was about the difficulty the small city of Albany was having finding qualified black administrators. To be fair, most of Albany's black and white residents viewed this particular newspaper as a rag, a tabloid, not a 'real' newspaper. But one has to wonder about the seven-year-old that has been practicing his reading skills. His parents are proud because their son has just been put into the advanced reading group in his school, the group that now practices reading stories aloud in front of the class. Imagine him, the sweet and curious little black boy strolling along the avenue and testing out his newly acquired reading skills. He passes by a stop sign and happily reads the word, "STOP." He glances at all of the signs posted on the windows of the grocery store, picks one and sounds out the words,

"G r r a a p e   F r r u i t s,   T h r e e   F o r a D o l l o r,"
and proudly gets it! "Grapefruits, Three For a Dollar!" the boy shouts exuberantly.

The boy then happens upon the newspaper stand which displays the paper nobody gives much credence to, but the little boy doesn't understand all of that because, after all, he's only seven years old and a newcomer to reading. He excitedly sounds out the words,

"N o In tel l i g e n t Bl a c k M e n Fo u n d H e r e"
He may or may not know what the word 'intelligent' means but he knows that there are none of whatever that word means where he lives in Albany. He continues on his way wondering, perhaps, what the newspaper said but not for long, because he has moved on to read signs that are perhaps easier to understand. When he gets home and boasts to his family about all of the things he can read he remembers the newspaper and asks the question,

"What does the word in tell i gent mean?"

"It means smart," his mom answers.

Then it hits him, what the words from the newspaper meant, the newspaper that he is unaware none of the adults care about. He translates this in his second grade brain to mean, 'No smart black men found here.' Later, at the dinner table that evening he asks his family,

"Is it true that there are no smart black men here?"

His dad looks at him somewhat incredulously. "Why in the world would you think that?"

"Because that's what the words on the newspaper said. Why did the newspaper say that? Is it true?"

A conversation then ensues about how wrong and ignorant the statement is and how you can't believe everything that you read in newspapers, and that that particular newspaper isn't a very good one. It may stop here because sometimes too much information can make the whole matter worse. The boy goes off to play hardly thinking much about the signs, the newspaper or passing by the grocery store. But in his absence, the rest of the family share openly with one another how they really feel about the newspaper's headline. They express frustration, anger and indignation that their seven-year-old had to be exposed at such an early age to such blatant racism.

The good news is that the seven-year-old will most likely not be too affected by this single event. He trusts and loves his family and he is secure and confident they have told him the truth. But he will continue to encounter more racism, blatant and subtle, throughout his life, and in the absence of proactive and positive racial socialization, the cumulative effect could be devastating. Devastating to his self-esteem and his beliefs about his own self-efficacy as well as the efficacy of his cultural group. And make no mistake, that devastation can and often will be passed on to his own children.

Racially socializing black children, teaching them about the strengths of their family and culture, along with the reality of discrimination and racism, gives them tools to emotionally and psychologically filter racist assaults against them personally and against black people as a group.

When black children are raised in an atmosphere of love and open communication about the world around them, a child like the one described above might come home, and after learning what the word 'intelligent' meant, assert, "I read something that was racist today."

A whole new discussion then happens as a result. Combating racism is no easy matter; just look at how big people are dealing with it. Consider the uproar about affirmative action, Native American land rights, and what to do about "those Arabs."

Everyone knows, even our children, that it is going to take more than a canned presidential speech or a good round of singing "We Are The

World" to fix the problem. So we should do ourselves and our children a favor by not pretending that the problem of racism no longer exists. We should not send them unprepared onto a racially charged battlefield ignorant of the mental, emotional and social landmines that await them. Little Tyrone should certainly not be told right out of diapers about what the statistical probability is that he will be arrested and serve jail time; or the likelihood that he may, based upon his name alone, be singled out and discriminated against. But telling black boys and girls about some of the problems which may face them, and how they might knowingly resolve them or avoid them seems the humane thing to do.

It is unfortunate that we have to teach our children to guard against anybody trying to touch their private parts, warn them not to talk to people that they do not know, and that not all grown-ups tell the truth or are good people. Regrettably, we have to protect our children from doing what comes naturally to them, being curious about their world and the people in it and trusting that they are safe and loved. As parents and adults, we are duty bound to guide and protect our children. As part of our covenant we must teach them how to navigate through the perils of our society's most deeply rooted discriminatory practices and still succeed.

Modeling

It is often said that the fastest way to learn a skill is to watch someone do it well and model yourself after them. Modeling is the chief way humans learn; especially when we are young. It is likely the most powerful educational tool we have. Most of us learn how to do life through the modeling of our parents and extended families. We learn how to parent, how to deal with money, how to be married, and how to be with our friends primarily through watching how those close to us do these things. The operative word here is watching.

If mom and dad fight a lot, their child will learn that fighting is part of being married. If mom and dad complain a lot about work, their child will learn that work is not meant to be enjoyed. If mom and dad save money and invest, that's what their child will learn to do with money. If mom and dad have rich spiritual lives, the chances are so will their children.

Young children will naturally learn almost any behaviors they repeatedly are exposed to. Therefore, we need to model the behaviors we want our children to exhibit. If you want your children to know right from wrong, you have to show them by your daily behavior. If you want them to be readers, they need to see you reading as part of your life. Whether or not you wish to be a model, if you have children, you are. Even if you don't have children, as long as you are around them you are a model. We must model those attributes we want them to learn.

So, in addition to sufficiently educating African Americans as to the social and cultural climate of their environment, we must also model a successful navigation through the well established minefield of racial intolerance. Through achieving moral and material successes we can go a long way towards destroying the myth of powerlessness and demonstrate, by example, how to accomplish life goals. It is important that in whatever venture we pursue, whether completing school, advancing in a career, or raising a healthy family, excellence should be the objective.

Modeling, (or the lack thereof) is why mere recitations like, 'Be all that you can be,' or pronouncements such as, 'You can do anything,' are not enough for African Americans, particularly for our children and youth. We need real, living and breathing examples. Without such examples, simple words of exhortation, seminars or more elaborate classes become chalked up to vague or idealistic hopes and dreams. People are often left discouraged and unconvinced. It is difficult to believe those around you that constantly tell you that your aspirations are definitely attainable when you don't know of anyone who has attained them. These real-life examples serve as evidence of possibility; and the more evidence in our immediate environment, the greater the expectation we will have of our own ultimate success.

Where do we find these exemplars, these successes who, in spite of the racism, in spite of the all the obstacles that most of us seem to face, have fulfilled their dreams? They are all around us; we just have to look. In many cases they are closer than we think. Often they are within our family. Sometimes they can be found in the family of a friend or community member. Wherever they are, find them, talk with them and learn from them.

Telling Our Story

Telling our stories can be redemptive. Telling our stories can free us. Telling our stories can help lift others up. I believe an integral part of racial socialization is learning the histories of those in our family and community. Story telling is an important part of our education; it strengthens us and helps us build resilience. It helps us put things in the proper perspective.

Why don't we do more of it? I believe two things tend to get in the way of African Americans telling their own stories and those about their parents and their parents' parents. I remember hearing a Jewish woman say that "surviving has not looked pretty" for many of us who have been oppressed.

It is clear that surviving and struggling as African Americans has often meant enduring tremendously demeaning and humiliating situations, remembered as shameful episodes not to be acknowledged or discussed. In efforts to move beyond the humiliation from past injustices, many of us have disassociated ourselves from the indignities that we or our relatives experienced in the struggle to prevail over slavery, systemic racist practices and poverty. Our failure to pass along these accounts of our familial past becomes a detriment to ourselves and our children.

Most parents want to ensure that their children will not have to struggle as they have struggled, so they work to provide their children with the support and resources necessary for them to avoid what they had suffered. I remember an incident involving a young athlete who had happened by my house He came to join up with my son for a game of basketball. As is customary in our home, I reminded my son that his chores needed to be completed before leaving the house, at which point the tall, lanky, neatly groomed visitor chuckled. The young man was wearing an expensive jogging suit, replete with matching Jordan basketball shoes that alone fetched a price of $135.00. A little perturbed, I asked him, "So what is it that you find so amusing about what I just said? I'm sure that you have chores to do at home!"

My husband entered the kitchen just in time to hear the young man's answer, "I don't have to do nothing at my house."

My husband tried, to no avail, to head me off from where he knew I was going next. He reminded me that this young man was not one of our offspring and that I should probably refrain from lecturing him. Unfortunately for the oblivious young visitor, my send button had already been pushed! I turned completely around and looked up into the barely pubescent face now smiling with pride for what he felt was both an honest and clever remark. I began by asking him about his mother who I knew was raising him on her own.

"Did your mother buy you the outfit that you have on?"

"Yes," he responded proudly.

"I'll bet that cost quite a bit of money."

"That's right." Still brimming with pride, the lights having not quite come on yet in my youthful guest.

I shared that I was aware of how hard his mother worked to feed and care for him and to keep him clothed in the way that he enjoyed. Slowly I could see a twinkling of awareness awaken in him. I explained that I knew that his mother would never want him to feel ashamed or to have to go without; that she worked extra hours to secure these popular 'must have' items. I asked him for his mother's sake and mine to never say that he 'did nothing' around the house to help her, and told him that she deserves much more from him.

I never heard him speak of the issue again. However, I doubt he spontaneously began creating chores for himself. I probably wouldn't be far off surmising that his mother may have felt ashamed as a young girl about not having nice clothes to wear and little time or resources for herself. It would not surprise me if she never sat her son down and told him her story, how she came to be who she is. If I am right, then by hiding her experience, her struggles, perhaps even her shame, and by not sharing with him the benefits that can be derived from life's hardships she was unwittingly stifling the son that she had striven to protect and encourage. What's more, he didn't get to truly appreciate the trials and adversities that she has undergone to raise him.

Our children are not aware of how, and who, endured what, in order for them to exist today. They have little knowledge of the struggles and suffering experienced by their forebears. Far too many black youth do not feel compelled to serve or give back in any way, even to the parents that have cared for them. They are historyless and ungrateful because they have been spared the details of their family's story. They move through the world lost from themselves. Randall Robinson has said that the worse thing that you could take from a people is "their memory of themselves." Our memories have been omitted from the history books. Worse still, they are absent from our family pictures and go undisclosed at our family reunions.

It is difficult, if not impossible, to instill a sense of pride and responsibility in African American children and youth when they remain ignorant about themselves. Black families have a wealthy store of memories about struggle, perseverance and victory, replete with the usual host of characters that are included in such accounts. The antagonists and villains along with the heroes and heroines provide colorful depictions of our family tapestry. We, the elders, have only to speak. We owe it to them to tell our stories and to encourage them to tell their own. By so doing we will build continuity across the generations, and with greater continuity will come a growing understanding of, and confidence in, our power to survive, overcome and flourish.

Moving Ahead: Building Upon Our Strengths

Building self-esteem, taking greater control of our inner world and racially socializing ourselves and our families are some of the steps we can take in order to heal from the effects of Post Traumatic Slave Syndrome. As we heal we also have to move ahead. To do so we can build upon traditional strengths that we have relied upon all along: our spirituality and faith, our sense of community and our tradition of great leaders. We have needed all of these and more to come as far as we have. Even with the limitations imposed by PTSS we have come a long way. We now can use these to help us complete the journey

Faith and Religion

The role of religion and faith in the survival of African slaves and their descendants is central and critical. African slaves arrived in America with varied religious beliefs stemming from differing cultural practices. It is estimated that as much as 20% of the slaves were Muslims; regardless of their religion, all were quickly indoctrinated into Christianity by white slave owners that viewed the religion of slaves as uncivilized and blasphemous. A great many of the original traditions and customs were lost. What did survive were the tribal stories about the ancestors and the strong rhythmic songs. These vestiges of African culture were eventually melded into the new Christian theology and emerged as a form of worship that can truly be considered uniquely African American.

When I was in graduate school I remember attending a forum in which students and faculty were dialoging about how to make the school of psychology more 'inclusive' and supportive of students. I raised my hand and asked why we never studied the role that faith has had in helping people to heal from psychological illness and distress. The room fell silent for a while and I continued, asking, "If we were to take the combined number of individuals successfully treated using the recognized theories of Freud,

Adler, Jung, Erikson, Bandura and others, would it equal the numbers of those who were able to restore their health through their faith?"

Still their was silence, so I proffered an answer and suggestion: "There are vast numbers of individuals all over the world who may or may not have any working knowledge of the famous theorists I just mentioned, yet would testify that their faith in God was what helped them. On numerical strength alone, it would appear sensible for this school to consider 'faith' as another viable approach to treatment."

It didn't go over well. They changed the topic and never got back to my question. This was particularly disconcerting and somewhat ironic given the fact that the field of psychology owes its roots to the study of the psyche, which is the Greek word meaning 'spirit' or 'soul.'

Separation of church and state, too politically charged or volatile, too difficult or impossible to measure, whatever their answer might have been, 'faith' as a healing agent remains as a quintessential paradox for those bastions of science committed to curing human ills. African Americans, however, are not and have never been deterred from placing a high value on their faith and turning to it for assistance and succor. If we are to become healthy, our deep commitment to God, spirituality and religion will be one of our primary building blocks.

The Spirit of Community

One of the beliefs that black people have been taught about themselves is that as a group they could and should not trust one another. Sowing the seeds of distrust was an important tool employed by slave owners as a way of preventing slave uprisings. In some cases this worked so well that some slaves would even alert the slave master to potentially troublesome slaves. If slaves shared a general distrust of one another, they were less prone to unite against a common enemy, namely the slave owners.

However, there was a time when black people would learn once again to trust and rely upon one another. This was during segregation, when Jim Crow laws legally separated blacks from whites, creating virtually two completely separate societies. Under Jim Crow legislation, the law allowed for segregation so long as the conditions for blacks were equal to that of whites. Despite the fact that the conditions were rarely, if ever at all equal, blacks managed to build a strong fortress of protection around themselves. The scars of slavery still lingered, but with the reconstruction of family and community the process of healing had begun. In some places black segregated towns excelled economically and socially, even beyond the towns of their white neighbors.

If Jim Crow segregation had fulfilled its promise of equality, African Americans, with no expectation of inclusion into white society, would likely have continued to prosper. In the absence of any other options we would have had to rely on and trust each other, live together, and eventually build a strong economic base. Had segregation fulfilled the promise of egalitarianism, it would have presented a chance for black people to learn once again that they could be self-sufficient, that they were capable of raising children who loved themselves, and that they could construct a community in which success was expected.

As we all know, Jim Crow was just codified oppression and simply that era's way of continuing our enslavement. The creation of two equal societies was the farthest thing from the minds of southern whites. America's version of Apartheid would have to be dismantled.

Integration became our new hope of equality and we fought long and hard for our civil rights. While some legal progress has been made since the days of Jim Crow, racial integration for African Americans has not been achieved to any appreciable degree. Given the 'progress' since Brown v Board of Education it would be a mistake to continue to wait and hope for justice and social and economic parity. We need to return to the days of building and relying upon our spirit of community.

In the past we have been able to accomplish great things through involving ourselves in our communities. We have created strong institutions, involved ourselves in social activism, delivered quality social services to those in need and provided mental, emotional and spiritual support and guidance for our own.

Regardless of how poor a community of black people are, churches are always sustained and supported. Today we have what has come to be known as the 'mega churches.' These churches have thousands of parishioners and monetary assets commensurate with the size of their congregations. Many of these churches have provided seed money to build homes and start businesses; they are active in social outreach, education, and other constructive efforts. Similar efforts have been made by the Muslim community as well as other faith-based groups.

Every year colleges and universities are graduating African American professionals in the areas of business, medicine, architecture, education, the arts, law and a variety of other fields. Black entrepreneurs are emerging to create corporations, establish philanthropic efforts, educate and support black children, youth and adults. Long-standing black organizations like the NAACP, United Negro College Fund, the National Urban League and the Black United Fund have all endeavored to invest in black communities in a myriad of ways. Of course we must not forget those countless unsung heroes who have toiled for long years in their communities seeking no recognition nor praise, who just rolled up their sleeves and, often unasked, did whatever work was needed.

To continue on the road to health we need our communities to regain their vibrancy and their relevancy. We need to begin to re-instill in ourselves and our children a sense of responsibility to others, to reinvent rites of passage that get beyond what is merely ceremonial. There are black communities around the country that have begun successful programs to reclaim their neighborhoods through collective action. It would be to our advantage if we were aware of what has successfully been done, as well as what is currently being done, so we can replicate and build upon these models. Randall Robinson has asserted that we as black people need a "Ministry of Information," that we are suffering from a lack of knowledge. This is true on many levels. I have often spoken of the need for a central clearing house where information can be disseminated nationally so to avoid reinventing the wheel locally. This clearing house could disseminate information about thriving ventures that involve everything from effective after school programs to commercial real-estate development. It can be a place where information is accessed and used to guide the replication of other fruitful efforts.

Establishing Strong Leadership

The African American community can no longer afford to have their collective voice silenced with a single shot! We can't look to a few individuals to provide guidance and direction. We must begin to look to ourselves for leadership. This is not to suggest that we ignore the leaders that we have, but rather to build communities of leaders so that the loss of one does not curtail for an instant our progress and growth.

Sadly, a fair number of our youths as well as adults are ignorant of many of our most important leaders. They do not understand the importance of black leadership and its role in determining their own futures because they remain unaware of individuals like Nathaniel Turner or Sojourner Truth. They have heard about Harriet Tubman and Frederick Douglass but have no knowledge of Marcus Garvey, Robert S. Abbott or W.E.B. Dubois. They celebrate Martin Luther King and Malcolm X but remain oblivious to the work of Angela Davis, Bobby Seale or Julian Bond. They know little of civil rights or the Harlem Renaissance and have no idea of how individuals like Frantz Fanon and Thurgood Marshall championed the struggle for civil and human rights amidst life-threatening circumstances. In short, an inexcusable number of us have grown up ignorant of our history and as a result are culturally bankrupt.

Unfortunately, many of those in leadership positions today fall short of what we need them to be. Again in a discussion with Mr. Robinson, when asked about black leadership, he responded by stating that unfortunately many of our black leaders had "come to do good, but stayed to do well." It is imperative that we hold those whom we consider as leaders accountable to us. In a similar vein, the late Maynard Jackson, former Mayor of Atlanta, said that we as black people have two major charges. First, we must address the "scared Negro" who gets placed in a position of power or leadership and becomes so afraid of losing his position that he will sell out the black support base that put him there. Second, we have to stop propping up incompetent leaders, because in doing so we lose our credibility as a group.

We need strong leadership in many areas: politics, jurisprudence, social activism, education, science, and business, to name a few. We need a community of leaders to expand our base of role models, show us paths to success, guide and mentor us. We need political and judicial leaders to keep up the fight for equal opportunity and access. We need social activist leadership to keep us on the path to community growth. We need leaders in education to expand the role and capacities of black educational institutions. We also need these leaders to guide students though high school, college and on through their advanced degrees. Perhaps most of all we need business leaders. We need business leaders who will mentor our people up the ladder of corporate America. We also need leaders who will return to our communities and aid in the creation of black-owned businesses.

We need our leaders to be men and women of principle. We need them to be courageous, audacious and humble servants. Most of all we need them to remain cognizant and respectful of their connection to those they would lead. If we are to develop a community of leaders we must educate them as well as hold them accountable. We must demand much from them and give them strong support in return. We have to ask some hard questions of those that would put themselves in leadership positions, and when the answers are to our liking, put all the resources we can muster behind them. That means we have to vote for black politicians who measure up. We have to send our children to schools that provide exemplary education. We have to support corporations with a track record of creating opportunities for African Americans and of supporting our communities. We especially have to support black-owned businesses. It is through our support that our leadership can grow to include us all.

Looking in the Mirror

Most of us want to create better lives for ourselves beyond meeting the basic survival needs. Rarely do we consider making better our 'character' as a way of improving our life. The task of becoming a better human is never ending (until, of course, 'the end').

When our youngest daughter was twelve, I noticed that the friends that she was attracting seemed to be self-centered and mean spirited. I suspected that my daughter had fallen victim to peer pressure, so I broached the subject of character. I shared with her that when I was in junior high school there were several different cliques that people belonged to. There were the popular kids, who always had the nicest clothes and knew the latest dances and music; the nerds, who were smart in class but lacked social skills; the tough kids, who were always in fights or bullying someone; the jocks, who were held in esteem because of their athletic skills; and the poor kids, who stayed to themselves to avoid becoming the brunt of jokes and teasing. The rest were the regular kids, who went unnoticed and wandered about the fringes of the other groups.

I asked my daughter who she was at school, what was her group? And was the person that she was at school consistent with the person that she was at home? She became noticeably uncomfortable and didn't offer an answer. She didn't have to, because it showed all over her face. I began to explain how I had at one point found myself surrounded by people whom I neither liked nor trusted and how I had to look at myself closely to determine what I had in common with them that had attracted them to me. I offered as an insight that I had to accept the fact that I had qualities that were in need of change and how difficult it was to remake myself. I told her how I decided to be a different person when I returned to school the next day, how no one believed the new Joy, and how they tried to involve me in the same old activities and behaviors, and how I refused to participate. After a couple of weeks they eventually stopped coming around and relegated me to the status of an 'outsider' and refused to speak to me. I was ecstatic! I felt free to be the new me.

She listened silently never saying a single word. The next day, a Saturday, she came to me and asked what was music to my ears,

"Mom, will you help me to make myself over?"

Thus, began her difficult and sometimes painful journey back to herself. I gave her a metaphor of a butterfly, explaining that she was now only a caterpillar frightened and crawling on the ground, but soon she would experience a metamorphosis. My daughter, now fully grown, has blossomed into the beautiful young woman that I always knew she was capable of being. And, to my chagrin, she has a bright, colorful tattoo of a butterfly on her back.

We all need to begin to re-examine our behaviors and our thoughts: how we speak to each other, how we treat each other, and how we show love. So much of what we do is ingrained and autonomic, a natural reflex of living. Someone who believes that they are affectionate may be unaware that they never tell their spouse or siblings that they love them, or offer an arm around the shoulder of a troubled friend. They may never demonstrate any vulnerability or acknowledge a personal weakness, and yet they are surprised when their children are indifferent to others' feelings, or find it impossible to admit when they are wrong.

The work ahead requires that we question some of our knee-jerk responses. We must question how we respond to other's achievements, and rather than being undermining or critical, we need to be elated and encouraging. We need to question how, or if, we need to defend ourselves from real or perceived insults, certain of our inherent worth. We need to re-examine how we mete out discipline and chastise our children, always careful to exercise temperance and wisdom rather than reverting to habits born from the fragmented remnants of a tortuous past. Perhaps most important of all, we as men and women, as families, neighbors, and communities, must increase our capacity to love and to assess whether or not our people, our culture, and our environment are made better as a result of our involvement.

Epilogue

Thomas Jefferson, one of America's most celebrated heroes, in a glaring and charged pronouncement acknowledged his guilt and fear with regard to the legacy of slavery. He bemoaned the plight of both races, the crippling of one people for the greed of commerce and in so doing abetting the lasting corruption of the other. This penned soliloquy stands as one of the greatest testimonies to the conscious and willful understanding by one of America's founding leaders, of the consequences of slavery, that bequeathed generations of physical and psychological suffering to America's future black citizenry, while it doomed America's white progeny to becoming the custodians of an invasive and pernicious racism.

> . . .*There must doubtless be an unhappy influence on the manners of our people produced by the existence of slavery among us. The whole commerce between master and slave is a perpetual exercise of the most boisterous passions, the most unremitting despotism on the one part, and degrading submissions on the other. Our children see this, and learn to imitate it; for man is an imitative animal. This quality is the germ of all education in him. From his cradle to his grave he is learning to do what he sees others do. If a parent could find no motive, either in his philanthropy or his self-love, for restraining the intemperance of passion towards his slave, it should always be a sufficient one that his child is present. But generally it is*

not sufficient. The parent storms, the child looks on, catches the lineaments of wrath, puts on the same airs in the circle of smaller slaves, gives a loose to his worst of passions, and thus nursed, educated, and daily exercised in tyranny, cannot but be stamped by it with odious peculiarities. The man must be a prodigy who can retain his manners and morals undepraved by such circumstances. And with what execration should the statesman be loaded, who permitting one half the citizens thus to trample on the rights of the other, transforms those into despots, and these into enemies, destroys the morals of the one part, and the amor patriae [love of country] of the other. For if a slave can have a country in this world, it must be any other in preference to that in which he is born to live and labour for another: in which he must lock up the faculties of his nature, contribute as far as depends on his individual endeavours to the evanishment of the human race, or entail his own miserable condition on the endless generations proceeding from him. With the morals of the people, their industry also is destroyed. For in a warm climate, no man will labour for himself who can make another labour for him. This is so true, that of the proprietors of slaves a very small proportion indeed are ever seen to labour. And can the liberties of a nation be thought secure when we have removed their only firm basis, a conviction in the minds of the people that these liberties are of the gift of God? That they are not to be violated but with his wrath? Indeed I tremble for my country when I reflect that God is just: that his justice cannot sleep for ever: that considering numbers, nature and natural means only, a revolution of the wheel of fortune, an exchange of situation, is among possible events: that it may become probable by supernatural interference! The Almighty has no attribute which can take side with us in such a contest. —But it is impossible to be temperate and to pursue this subject through the various considerations of policy, of morals, of history natural and civil. We must be contented to hope they will force their way into

everyone's mind. I think a change already perceptible, since the origin
of the present revolution. The spirit of the master is abating, that of
the slave rising from the dust, his condition mollifying, the way I hope
preparing, under the auspices of heaven, for a total emancipation, and
that this is disposed, in the order of events, to be with the consent of
the masters, rather than by their extirpation.

Thomas Jefferson, *Notes on the State of Virginia, 1781* [70]

Upon this 'total emancipation' hoped for and still yet to be realized, depends the welfare of America. What chance can there be for our nation's lasting peace when the members of our own households are at war? A war fueled by ignorance, and powered by hatred and greed? How can a people be said to be free when so many are still held captive by poverty, fear and grief? Like Jefferson, I also tremble, but not with fear. I tremble with eager anticipation of change, and with a profound certainty of victory. The trembling is my heart's voice thundering the call from the 'door of no return' to the charred ruins of Tulsa and the blood stained churches of Birmingham, a call that can only have one answer: "Justice."

Let the Healing Begin!

Acknowledgments

I would like to acknowledge and thank my family, friends, my Baha'i community, and colleagues who stood by me, guided and supported me in writing this book. I could not have made it through without your encouragement and faith in the work.

Suggested Readings

Akbar, N. (1990). *Chains and Images of Psychological Slavery*. New Jersey: New Mind Productions.

Allen, J., Als, H., J. Lewis, & L. F. Litwack. (2000). *Without Sanctuary: Lynching Photography in America*. New Mexico: Twin Palms Publishers.

Asante, M. K., & K. W. Asante. (1985). *African Culture: The Rhythms of Unity*. Westport, CN: Greenwood Press.

Bell, C. C., & J. E. Jenkins. (1991). Traumatic Stress and Children. *Journal of Health Care for the Poor and Underserved, 2 (1)175-188*

Butterfield, F. (1995). *All God's Children: The Bosket Family and the American Tradition of Violence*. New York: Avon Books

Byrd, A. D., L. L. Tharps, (2001). *Hair Story: Untangling the Roots of Black Hair in America*. New York: St. Martin's Press.

Cole, D. (1999). *No Equal Justice: Race and Class in the American Criminal Justice System*. New York: The New Press.

Danieli, Y. (1998). *International Handbook of Multigenerational Legacies of Trauma*. New York: Plenum Press.

Gatto, J. T.(1992). *Dumbing Us Down*. Philadelphia, PA: New Society.

Genovese, E. D. (1976). *Roll Jordan Roll: The World the Slaves Made*. New York: Vintage Books.

Ginzburg, R. (1988). *100 Years of lynching*. Baltimore, MD: Black Classic Press.

Grier, W. H., & P. M. Cobbs. (1969). *Black Rage*. New York: Bantam Books.

Gutman, H. G. (1976). *The Black Family in Slavery and Freedom 1750-1925*. New York: Vintage Books.

Hacker, A. (1992). Two Nations: Black and white, separate, hostile, unequal. New York, NY: Macmillan publishing Company.

Kapsalis, T. (1997) *Public Privates: Performing Gynecology From Both Ends of the Speculum.* Durham, NC: Duke University Press.

Leary J. D., Brennan, E. & Briggs, H. (2005). African American Respect Scale - A Measure of a Prosocial Attitude. *Research on Social Work Practice.*

Mazrui, A. A. (1986). *The African: A Triple Heritage.* Boston: Little, Brown and Company.

Mbiti, J. (1970). *African Religions and Philosophy.* New York: Doubleday.

Miller, D. B. & R. MacIntosh. (1999). Promoting Resilience in Urban African American Adolescents: Racial Socialization and Identity As Protective Factors. *Social Work Research. 23 (3), 159-169.*

Morris, T. (1996). *Southern Slavery and the Law, 1619-1860.* Chapel Hill, NC: The University of North Carolina Press

National Spiritual Assembly. (1991). *The Vision of Race Unity: America's Most Challenging Issue.* Wilmette, Il: Baha'i Publishing Trust

Nichols, E. J. (1976). *Introduction to the Axiological Model.* Paper Presented to the World Psychiatric Association and the Nigerian Association of Psychiatrists. University of Ibadan, Nigeria.

Ogbu, J. U. (1990). Racial Stratification and Education. In G. E. Thomas (Ed.) *U. S. Race Relations in the 1980's and 1990's: Challenges and Alternatives.* New York: Hemisphere Publishing Company.

Osofsky, G. (1969). Puttin'on Ole Massa. New York: Harper Torch Books.

Pinderhughes, E. (1989). Understanding Race, Ethnicity, and Power. New York: The Free Press.

Poussaint, A. F. & A. Alexander. (2000). *Lay My Burden Down: Unraveling Suicide and the Mental Health Crisis among African Americans.* Boston, MA. Beacon Press.

Roberts, D. (1999). *Killing the Black Body.* New York: Vintage Books.

Robinson, R. (2004). *Quitting America: The Departure of a Black Man From His Native Land.* New York: Dutton.

Robinson, R. (2000). *The Debt: What America Owes to Blacks.* New York: Penguin.

Stevenson, H. C. (1994). Racial Socialization in African American Families: The Art of Balancing Intolerance and Survival. *The Family Journal: Counseling Therapy for Couples and Families. 2 (3), 190-198.*

Stevenson, H. C. (1994). Relationship of Adolescent Perceptions of Racial Socialization to Racial Identity. *Journal of Black Psychology. 21 (1) 49-70*

Tatum, B. D. (1997). *Why Are All the Black Kids Sitting Together in the Cafeteria?* New York: Basic Books.

Universal House of Justice. (1985). *The Promise of World Peace.* Wilmette, Il: Baha'i Publishing Trust

West, C. (1993). *Race Matters.* Boston, MA: Beacon Press.

Williams, J. (1998). *Thurgood Marshall: American Revolutionary.* New York: Times Books.

Winbush, R. A. (2001). *Should America pay?* New York, Harper Collins Books.

References

1. King, J. The Biology of Race. Los Angeles: University of California Press, 1981. p. 118.

2. Asante, M. K., & Asante, K. W. African culture: The rhythms of unity. Westport, CN: Greenwood Press. 1985. p. 31.

3. Mbiti, J. African religions and philosophy. New York: Doubleday 1970. p. 64.

4. Dowie, M. Pinto Madness. Mother Jones Magazine . Sept/Oct 1977. pp. 18-22.

5. Morris, T. Southern slavery and the law, 1619-1860. Chapel Hill, NC: The University of North Carolina Press. 1996. pp. 8-19

6. Madison, J. Federalist Papers, #54. 1788.

7. Day, P. J. A New History of Social Welfare. New Jersey: Prentice Hall, 1989. p. 148.

8. Webster's Ninth New Collegiate Dictionary, Springfield, MA: Merriam Webster, 1983.

9. Haller, J. S. Outcasts From Evolution. Chicago, IL: Illinois Press. 1971.p. 4.

10. Ibid, p. 5.

11. Ibid, p. 5.

12. Peterson, M. The portable Thomas Jefferson: Notes on the State of Virginia, 1781. New York: Viking Press. 1975. pp.192-193.

13. Ibid, p.193.

14. Madison, J. Federalist Papers, #54. 1788.

15. State of Virginia Casual Killing Act, 1669.

16. Cobb, T. R. R. An Inquiry into the Law of Negro Slavery in the United States of America. Savannah, GA: 1858. pp. 46-47.

17. Fowler, O. S., & L. N. Fowler. 1859. *The self-instructor in phrenology and physiology: with over one hundred new illustrations, including a chart for the use of practical phrenologists.* Revised by Nelson Sizer. New York, NY: Fowler and Wells. pp. 64-65.

18. Gould, S. J., *The Mismeasure of Man.* 1996. New York, NY: W.W. Norton and Co.

19. Curtain, P. 1969. *The Atlantic Slave Trade A Census.* Madison, WI: University of Wisconsin Press.

20. Thomas, H. 1997. *The Slave Trade: The Story of the Atlantic Slave Trade, 1440-1870.* New York, NY: Touchstone. p. 804

21. Morris, T. 1996. *Southern slavery and the law, 1619-1860.* Chapel Hill, NC: The University of North Carolina Press. pp. 305-306.

22. Roberts, D. 1997. *Killing the Black Body: Race, Reproduction an the Meaning of Liberty.* New York, NY: Vintage Books. pp. 29-30.

23. Kapsalis, T. *Public Privates: Performing Gynecology From Both Ends of the Speculum.* Durham, NC. Duke University Press. 1997. p. 41.

24. State of Oregon Constitution, 1859. (repealed November 3, 1926)

25. State of Oregon Constitution, 1859. (Repealed June 28, 1927)

26. McLagan, E. 1990. *A Peculiar Paradise a History of Blacks in Oregon, 1788-1940.* Portland, OR: Georgian Press. p. 31.

27. Bennett, L. 1971. *Pictorial History of Black America.* Chicago, IL: Johnson Publishing.

28. Mancini, M. J. 1996. *One Dies, Get Another: Convict Leasing in the American South, 1866-1928.* University of South Carolina Press, Columbia, S.C.

29. Butterfield, F. 1995. *All God's Children: The Bosket Family and the American Tradition of Violence.* New York, NY: Avon Books.

30. Ellwood, C. A. 1913. *Sociology and Modern Social Problems.* New York, NY: American Book Company. p. 252.

31. King, M. L. 2005. *Why We Can't Wait.* East Rutherford, NJ: Penguin. p. 29. (Originally published 1964)

32. Hymowitz, C. & Weissman, M. 1980. *A History of Women in America.* New York, NY: Bantam Books.

33. Davis, R. L. F. "Creating Jim Crow: In Depth Essay." http://www.jimcrowhistory.org/history/creating2.htm (21 November 2004)

34. Wells-Barnett, I. B. 1900. Lynch Law in America. *The Arena 23.1:* 15-24.

35. Wells-Barnett, I. B.

36. Bennett, L. J. 1966. *Before the Mayflower: A History of the Negro in America,* Chicago, IL: Johnson Publishing Co. p. 294.

37. Ginzburg, R. 1962. *100 Years of Lynching.* Baltimore, MD: Black Classic Press. p. 12.

38. Staples, B. 1999. "Unearthing a Riot." *New York Times Magazine, December 19:* pp. 64-69.

39. Staples, B.

40. Westley, R. 2003. "Black Reparations as Precondition to Civil Equality." In *Should America Pay? Slavery and the Raging Debate on Reparations.,* Edited by. R. A. Winbush. New York, NY: Harper Collins. p. 132.

41. Hacker, A. 1992. *Two Nations: Black and White, Separate, Hostile, Unequal.* New York, NY: Macmillan Publishing Company. p. 3.

42. Hacker, A. p. 4.

43. Carnevale, A. P. 2005. "The Affirmative Action No One Speaks Of." *The Chronicle of Higher Education. Jan. 13, 2005.* Transcript of live colloquy. http://chronicle.com/colloquy/2005/01/faculty/ (27 April 2005)

44. Bertrand, M. & S. Mullainathan. 2003 "Are Emily and Greg More Employable than Lakish and Jamal? A field Experiment on Labor Market Discrimination." *National Bureau of Economic Research, Working Paper No. 9873.* July

45. Bureau of Labor: "Unemployed Persons by Marital Status, Race, Age, and Sex." http://www.bls.gov/cps/cpsaat24.pdf (22 March 2005)

46. Lerman, R. I. 1997. "Meritocracy without Rising Inequality? Wage Rate Differences Are Widening by Education and Narrowing by Gender and Race." http://www.urban.org/urlprint.cfm?ID=6393 (22 March 2005)

47. Coffey, D. 1998. *Encyclopedia of the Vietnam War: A Political, Social, and Military History.* Ed. Spencer C. Tucker. Oxford, UK:ABC-CLIO.

48. Cole, D. 1999. *No Equal Justice: Race and Class in the American Criminal Justice System.* New York, NY: The New Press. p. 5.

49. Leonhardt, D. "As Prison Labor Grows; So Does the Debate." New York Times on the Web. Mar. 2000. http://www.fedcrimlaw.com/visitors/PrisonLore/prison-labor.html. (10 May 2005)

50. Hitt, J. 2003. Does America Owe a Debt to the Descendants of Its Slaves? In *Should America Pay? Slavery and the Raging Debate on Reparations,*. Edited by R. A. Winbush. New York, NY: Harper Collins. p. 107.

51. Palast, G. 2002. The Great Florida Election Ex-Con Game: How the 'felon' voter-purge was itself felonious. *Harpers Magazine. Mar. 1.*

52. American Psychiatric Association (1994). *Diagnostic and Statistical Manual of Mental Disorders. (4ᵗʰ edition).* Washington, DC.

53. American Psychiatric Association

54. Comer, J. P. 1980. *The Black Family: An Adaptive Perspective.* Unpublished manuscript, Yale University Study Center. p. 47.

55. Danieli, Y. 1998. *International Handbook of Multigenerational Legacies of Trauma.* New York, NY: Plenum Press. p. 9.

Index